BERKSHIRE

Edited by Simon Harwin

First published in Great Britain in 2003 by
YOUNG WRITERS
Remus House,
Coltsfoot Drive,
Peterborough, PE2 9JX
Telephone (01733) 890066

HB ISBN 0 75434 289 1
SB ISBN 0 75434 290 5

Foreword

This year, the Young Writers' The Write Stuff! competition proudly presents a showcase of the best poetic talent from over 40,000 up-and-coming writers nationwide.

Young Writers was established in 1991 and we are still successful, even in today's modern world, in promoting and encouraging the reading and writing of poetry.

The thought, effort, imagination and hard work put into each poem impressed us all, and once again, the task of selecting poems was a difficult one, but nevertheless, an enjoyable experience.

We hope you are as pleased as we are with the final selection and that you and your family continue to be entertained with *The Write Stuff! Berkshire* for many years to come.

CONTENTS

The Poems

My Pet . . .

Is a pig
I like my pig
He is fat
My mum likes my pig
My dad hates my pig
My pig can be good
My pig can be bad
The pig is pink
He is a very fast runner
The pig had too much to eat
He had to sleep it off.

Mary Driscoll (14)

Swaps

I'll give you . . .

A toy monkey
A green parrot
Mushroom coloured sweatshirt
Young tortoise
A gold watch
Lots of gold jewellery
A toy frog
A toy boat
A pet cat
A pet dog
For your KitKat
What do you say?
Yes.

Daniel Wood (15)
Addington School

Swaps

I'll give you . . .
Twenty-five bars of chewing gum
A new pair of jeans
A new pink T-shirt
A diamond ring
A watch with a metal strap
Some golden earrings
A pearl necklace
Size nine black shoes
And a CD player
For your Galaxy
What do you say?
Yes!

Thomas Beale (14)
Addington School

Swaps

A digger
A garden centre
A week's supply of chocolate
A train ticket to Reading and back
A limo
A hot air balloon ride
A punch in the face
A year's supply of CDs
A pair of Nike classics
For your Twix.
What do you say?
No!

Richard Thorpe (14) & Wayne Knight (15)
Addington School

Swaps

I'll give you . . .
A Dime bar
A packet of Fruit Pastille sweets
A trip on holiday to somewhere hot
In America, like Las Vegas
A new Harley Davidson
A new car - a BMW
A new computer
A new house
A flower
A CD
A nice snowy day
For your Mars bar
What do you say?
Yes!

Ben Reilly (15)
Addington School

Gardening

G ate made of chocolate.
A nts needing an atlas.
R abbits ride on lawnmowers.
D ogs barking madly at the
E quipment in the shed.
N oisy neighbours nesting
I n a begonia tree.
N oisy, noisy hot summers in our
G arden den.

Daniel Bennett (14)
Castle School

HOLIDAY POEM

H ave fun
O n holiday
L ying in the sun
I ce cream on a
D ay in Bournemouth
A way from
Y esterday's work.

Hayley Dunstan (14)
Castle School

HOLIDAY

H ad fun
O n my bike saw a
L adybird
I n the garden
D id have some fun
A nd
Y elled hooray.

Carla Barnes (13)
Castle School

GARDENING

My favourite job is gardening
I crash and bang and make a din
I dig up weeds and plant my seeds
I grow enough to fill my needs.

Anthony Williams (14)
Castle School

HOLIDAY

H ousework
O n my bike it was fun
L aughing
I ce cream
D rove to Thatcham
A lways with my friend
Y esterday.

Carol Watson (12)
Castle School

DOG

My dog is barking at the cat,
His long nose hitting the fishing net
He is fast at running after cats
He has black and brown long hair
It is in a knot all sticky and smelly.

Gavin Barnes (14)
Castle School

FEEL IT

I feel with my hands,
I feel cold water and warm.
Strange feel of paint,
I hate the feel of a jumper or something slimy,
I like feeling lumpy stuff with my feet.

Keith Black (14)
Castle School

THE FALLS . . .

As the day begins, the falls switch on
Gliding and sliding, slowly at first
Becoming rapid, but gently
Pebbles and rocks below, scattered with jewels
Which droplets leave behind
Falling from high above, comes the fall
Transforming into a graceful ripple at its end.

The day progresses and so do the falls,
So soft, so pure from start to finish
Great leaps leave a delicate layer of froth
Clear water creates the colourless falls
So clear like the midday air.

As the sun sets
The falls become tired
They talk to the passing wind
Wave to the flying birds
Gradually, slowing down
They prepare for the night
As they glitter like diamonds
In the glowing moonlight.

Rakhee Daggar (14)
Churchmead CE (VA) School

MY FAVOURITE THINGS

Flowers in summer breezes,
Lambs in hopping stages,
Kittens that play so happily in the newborn seasons,
Babies giggling and smiling, these make me happy.

People so friendly and kind,
Girls and boys playing happily,
Doggies and hamsters, so cute and cuddly
The first days of spring, these make me happy.

Samantha Blakemore (11)
Churchmead CE (VA) School

Down By The River

River ripples
Fish splash
Trade them in for dirty cash.

Fishing far
Chilling out
Is just what fishing's all about.

Cool rods
Awesome floats
People fish off their boats.

Trout tench
Vicky's bridge
Save your maggots in the fridge.

Hot and sunny
Cold and wet
Catch some fish in your net.

Let's go home
That's what's right
Wait a minute I've got a bite.

Daniel Plummer (14)
Churchmead CE (VA) School

My Pet Dog

S ammy is the name of my puppy.
A Labrador her breed is.
M y puppy is the sweetest thing.
M ental sometimes she can be.
Y ucky food she eats.

M ud is what she rolls in.
Y esterday she chased a bird.

P edigree Chum she eats.
E ating is her favourite thing.
T oppling over stairs.

D ucks she chases after.
O ver and out she goes all day.
G ates are what she jumps over.

Divya Daggar (12)
Churchmead CE (VA) School

Bedroom

B ed is where I sleep.
E very day I go to my bedroom.
D ays go by and it remains the same.
R ules don't apply here.
O ne likes his room.
O ver time it gets messy.
M y bedroom is my living space.

David Faulkner (12)
Churchmead CE (VA) School

JEM

Jem is a little rascal,
She bites my other cat's neck,
So they get in a fight
And Marley always wins!
Jem's favourite toy is a bottle cap,
She carries it around in her mouth,
Bats it about a bit like a mouse.
Jem will jump up on your lap.
She won't stay so she lap swaps.
We try to get her in for the night.
She runs so we don't follow.
Jem never makes up her mind.
Marley has no food 'til she makes up her mind.
Jem tries to eat the fish on the side.
She also helps you eat your food on the table.

Lucy Grant (12)
Churchmead CE (VA) School

AUTUMN DAYS

A utumn days are fun
U mbrellas being used when rain comes down
T rees are losing their leaves rapidly
U sing the blanket, hiding my face
M y mother gives me a cup of hot chocolate
N o one dares to go outside

D ays have gone by quickly
A utumn is finishing now
Y es snow will be falling
S nowy weathers now have started.

Zeenat Fayaz (12)
Churchmead CE (VA) School

An Autumn Day

The wind blows the scattered leaves,
Which fall from the nearly leafless trees.
They blow around the newly cut grass,
Orange, red, green, brown and yellow,
Whirlwinds of colours scatter and crumble.
The wind wraps a cold chill around the people of the street,
As they shiver and pull their winter coats about them.
They trudge on with their daily business,
Wishing they were snuggled up warm,
Next to the orange glowing fire inside the brightly lit room.
The sky looks cloudy as if the heavens
Are about to open and shower down on us.
Autumn, the most colourful season ever.

Louise Richardson (12)
Churchmead CE (VA) School

My Friends

M is for mad, which they are
Y is for yellow, one of my friends fave colours

F is for funny, they all are
R is for rows we mostly have
I is for ice cream our fave food
E is for endless fun we always have
N is for nutty, they sometimes are
D is for days when we always see each other
S is for silly when we are all there.

Michelle Snelling (12)
Churchmead CE (VA) School

The Mountain Bikes

The rider rides as fast as he can
Jumps as high as a tree
Over a tabletop
Jump success . . .
Skids the corner
Wheelspins away
The wild crowd cheer
But then
Suddenly . . .
He hits a bump in the trail
He falls
He goes over the handlebars
Hits the charcoal dirt
He's now in first
Now he's won the grand final.

Mark Kent (14)
Churchmead CE (VA) School

Best Friend

B est friend
E xtremely kind
S onia is her name
T he bestest friend ever

F un to be with
R eally nice
I s always there
E astEnders is our favourite soap
N ever nasty
D ogs she loves.

Intikhab Akhtar (12)
Churchmead CE (VA) School

My Car

Rubber burns
Quick like the wind
Fast as a cheetah
Ripping the road
Air hitting my face
Smashing the air into tiny pieces as it whizzes by
Sleek as sunset
Black as the night
A stallion on the long windy road
Windows rolled down
Soft leather
Hair in my face
Mysterious as a shadow
We fly through the night.

Avneet Chana (13)
Churchmead CE (VA) School

My Life

G eorge is my name
E mma is my ex-girlfriend
O range is my favourite fruit
R abbits, I have one
G oats are ugly
E lephants are enormous

C ats are my worst pet
A ccidents make me shiver
R oast dinners, I hate them
T he West Ham midfielder Joe Cole is my favourite player
E very day I play football
R at Race is my favourite film.

George Carter (12)
Churchmead CE (VA) School

WHAT MY NAME CAN SAY

L ike texting people
U nusual taste in clothes
C loud nine exists, I think
Y um, I like chocolate

P robably annoying
R eally giggly
O bviously talented
U nlucky
D aring
L ovely sense of humour
O f course I'm special
C aring
K ind.

Lucy Proudlock (12)
Churchmead CE (VA) School

FEELINGS

As a sense of responsibility and sympathy
The muscle pumps endlessly
As pounding thunderstorms
You feel hurt and overwhelmed
But the heart goes on descending
A companionable friend
Keeping partnership in your mortality
But yet soft, gentle and mild
With a sense of fatality
My friend keeps me alive
Keeps me dreaming
The closest relationship is
Between everlasting feeling.

Ritika Sharma (13)
Churchmead CE (VA) School

MYSTERIOUS WATERS

Mystic and dark the waters shook
The fish were rising to feed
Colours spread like a wildfire
Burning ambers and crimson reds
Shining scales and flashing fins
Water boiled as they twisted and turned
And leapt to sate their need
Rings of passion, hunger and fear
Darting for cover as a shadow appeared
The fearful form of a heron
Beneath the lilies they hide away
Until their foe had gone, they would not stray
Night falls, the fish have gone
Returning to their party down under
Darkness sets, the fish living their life
But that's another story.

Andrew Rolland (13)
Churchmead CE (VA) School

AUTUMN DAYS

A utumn is now here
U mbrellas go up when it rains
T he wind blows and makes me shiver
U sing the radiator to keep me warm
M y kettle's boiled to make me tea
N o one dares to go outside

D ays have gone by so fast
A utumn days are nearly over
Y ummy hot food ready for me
S nowy weather is now next.

Rebecca Wimpenny (12)
Churchmead CE (VA) School

The Terrible Storm

Lightning shot down like a bullet
Towards your head,
The wind screamed with anger.
Waiting for all this to stop.
Splish splash, you could hear the rain coming down.
There was no sign of light.
Clouds filled with misty black colours.
It was as cold as a mountain top.
At last a silver ray of sun escaped.
The black clouds shifted,
A rainbow spread itself across the sky.
We all smiled.

Chiranjeev Chaggar (12)
Churchmead CE (VA) School

Kiran Nandra

K iran is my name.
I love ice cream.
R unning is not my best.
A rt is my best lesson.
N aughty my mum believes I am.

N andra is my surname.
A pples are my favourite fruit.
N ana is the best member of my family.
D rama is my second best lesson.
R hyming poems is my worst nightmare.
A ction films are my favourite.

Kiranjyot Kaur Nandra (12)
Churchmead CE (VA) School

BASKETBALL

Dodging out of the way,
As the ball is thrown into view.

It whizzed past my ear like a bird of prey.
The opponents rush for the ball
Like a pack of lions scrambling for their kill.
Whoosh!

I jumped up and tried to shoot.
The adrenaline was pumping through my veins.

Thoughts were running through my mind,
Figuring out what to do next.
Suddenly I saw the ball flying *up! Up! Up!*

Going
Down, down, down,
And through the hoop . . . *score!*
My teammates cheered at me,
The spectators called me the man of the match.
Our opponents had been defeated.

Anil Sharma (13)
Churchmead CE (VA) School

9/11

He is running, he's running
As fast as he can.
He wants to help them,
He's a fireman.

Jumping from the building,
It's very high.
At the end of the day
People will die.

The building's collapsed,
People are running away.
People are trying to help,
They'll try every day.

The day is over,
The place is deserted.
Everyone's indoors,
The place is converted.

Robert Bourne (13)
Churchmead CE (VA) School

Sunset

Sleeping Beauty,
Waiting to be tucked in,

Lovers' Hill, always packed,

People, waiting, waiting,
For sun to settle,
Darkness to fall,

Flittering, fluttering birds
Drawn towards her,
Like a moth to a flame,

Radiant beams of light,
Shine onto the deep blue sea,

Twinkling twilight dazzles people's eyes,
Filling the sky with shimmering sparkles,

Crisp golden outline begins to fade,
Dusk approaches,
The night is here.

Vicki Norcott (13)
Churchmead CE (VA) School

My Mum

My mum is as sweet as sugar
She always helps me out,
Whenever I'm in trouble
She'll always be about.

My mum's name is Gill
She loves to watch football,
Her favourite team is Arsenal,
Against Chelsea they drew two all.

My mum is getting old now,
An age I cannot say,
But she acts like she's twenty
All night and all day.

And now it's time to celebrate
How nice my mum can be,
I really do love my mum
As you all can see!

Kim Woodward (12)
Churchmead CE (VA) School

Rainbows

Rainbows are so pretty
Rainbows are so bright
Rainbows come in different colours
Red, yellow, pink or green, orange and purple and blue
Rainbows are so colourful and pretty
Rainbows are so beautiful
Rainbows come from the rain
I love rainbows and I love the rain.

Aamina Bashir (11)
Churchmead CE (VA) School

FAMILY CELEBRATION

There's a celebration at this house
A family one at that
It might be a wedding or a birthday
We do not know for a fact.

There's a celebration at this house
One of my friends of course
His name is James
And he likes to watch Inspector Morse.

There's a celebration at this house
One of my cousins I think
He does not like my little pet mouse
But now he is playing on his V-tech link.

Ellis Bordessa (12)
Churchmead CE (VA) School

FEELINGS OF AUTUMN

If you are sad,
Look at the autumn leaves
Marching,
The flowers singing,
Birds talking,
Butterflies dancing,
The crisp clean skies,
Air cuddling,
Skies so low,
Earth embracing,
Just put a swing in your feet
And start smiling.

Taranum Bawa (12)
Churchmead CE (VA) School

FOOTBALL

Green blades of grass
Like sharp ridged knives

Shouting crowds
Like a stampede of rhinos

Black and white football
As round as an apple

Lightning football players
Like a fast train speeding off

Hard goals
Like missiles coming out of a launcher.

Rizwaan Pinjara (12)
Churchmead CE (VA) School

FOOTBALL

Round football
As shiny as the moon

Loud ref
Shouting like a lion

Anxious net
Like a shark waiting for its prey

Tired team
Sleepy as a koala

Roaring crowd
Hollering like a stampede of buffaloes.

Mark Louder (12)
Churchmead CE (VA) School

CRICKET

Stripy lawn
like a camouflage of a tiger

Round ball
like the spinning Earth

Players out
like a life cycle of a human

Willow bat
like an echo in a mountain

The motionless umpire
like the Statue of Liberty.

Harmeet Jagdev (12)
Churchmead CE (VA) School

FISHING

Sharp shiny hook
like Captain Hook's hand in the panto

Swim for standing on
like being in a huge puddle

Sparkling river
like a bottle of bubbly champagne

Bright line
like a glistening stone

Smooth reel
like a bike wheel going round.

Lenny Fletcher (12)
Churchmead CE (VA) School

KNOCKOUT!

Assassinating a punch,
As a high-flying attack hits me,
Bang!
I fall to the floor,
Excited spectators wait anxiously
For me to get up,
I see large shadowy figures
In my head.
I wake up.
Look around
And I become
A warrior,
Once again.

Nikhil Sharma (13)
Churchmead CE (VA) School

FOOTBALL

Green pitch
as neat as my paper

Noisy crowd
as loud as a train

Strict ref
as hard as an English teacher

Beaming floodlights
as bright as car lights

Round football
like a planet in the sky.

Jemal Hussein (12)
Churchmead CE (VA) School

Mist

A dust cloud over the town
Grey, dull, hazy
Everything blurred like a blind man's vision
Tired, sleepy, sad
Moaning as it passes houses
Vapour, spray, steam
Breathing leaving steam on windows
Film, net, tissue
No one could escape once inside
Dew, drizzle, drops
Laughing spit flew out
Crept, slowly, silently
Creeping up on houses *'Boo!'*
Thick, coated, dense
Like a jigsaw of slate tiles
The mist moans and groans.

Orwa Hameed (13)
Churchmead CE (VA) School

Snake's Slither

Snake slithers in the late hour
With its scary skin so white
It's like an ice pole
It can be captured and can be told
With its tongue so long it can be used as a gun
Hanging from tree to tree it watches its prey
Comes down and squeezes its head
Until it rips it off
It swallows it whole.

Bilaal Rawn (13)
Churchmead CE (VA) School

MOTORCROSS

Motorbikes revving as loud as a lion roaring,
The flag goes down,
People fly like rockets around the first corner,
Parents thinking, has my son fell off or not?
All you see in your eyes is dust,
All I'm thinking, am I first or last?
No, I have just run something over.
I look behind, it was my friend's front tyre.
He gets back on, thank goodness,
I see two people in front. I must be third,
Thank goodness I'm not last,
As I go around the last corner all I see are parents
Cheering at the top of their voices,
But parents are looking for their sons,
The children thinking, am I last? Feeling guilty,
Better luck next time.

Lewis Horsted (12)
Churchmead CE (VA) School

A STORM

The clouds play like a little child,
As the lightning strikes it's mild,
The trees scream when their leaves fall,
The storm starts to brew and wail,
As thunder booms like it's World War II,
The rain falls and gets stronger too,
Children scream as the thunder strikes,
Parents tell them not to panic, it'll be over soon,
As the storm passes over,
Children say, 'Thank goodness that's over!'

Jason Myers (12)
Churchmead CE (VA) School

Dangerous Sport

Sport can be a dangerous thing,
Formula 1 is the worst,
Because you could be first,
Then comes a car
And before you know it, you could be in the barrier,
Just like a moth to a flame,
Then you'll be the one to blame,

You can drive a car,
Like it was the machine of the season,
If you win, the car is the reason,
Racing can be a killer,
Just like Ayrton Senna found his car was a spinner,
Cars take-off like a scolded cat,
Then you turn the corner, you can't see
You're as blind as a bat,

Your car is badly worn out,
You'll be up out of the cockpit,
Hopefully up and about
And your car in one bit,
The marshall is waving a yellow flag,
You're disappointed like a worn out old bag,
Another race has gone, you haven't won,
But next time you'll be spraying champagne,
Having a lot of fun.

Nathan Sharpe (13)
Churchmead CE (VA) School

BSX (Mountain Biking)

The trail was a virgin,
With only one person upon it,
He zigzags through the trees of the woods,
Wheels carve the ground like razor blades,
His tyre slides,
He's flung through the air,
Rocks jump to dodge his falling body.
Wallop! He hits the mud,
But he's back on his feet,
As he glides over the uneven ground,
His shocks aid his ride.
Logs duck as his wheels swirl out of control,
The bike soars through the air over the camel humps,
He swings round his back wheel to pull off a trunk *bash,*
Pedals spin as his foot slips,
He yanks his front brake and is endoed to the heavens,
As he hits the floor twigs scream,
'That's enough!' he yells.
He limps away,
Bike a crumpled heap on the ground,
The bike groans,
Trees settle down,
Stones stay put and feels safe,
Whilst logs wander off down the hill,
The rider picks up his bike and rides off awkwardly.

Thomas Lansley (13)
Churchmead CE (VA) School

THE VIEW FROM MY BEDROOM WINDOW

As I wake in the early hours of the morn
I can hear the singing of all the beautiful birds in the sky,
All the colours of their wings and feathers, their bright, colourful beaks.
Their feathers are as bright as a rainbow on a cloudy day.
As the birds tweet the sun rises and it's a joy to hear them
Play together in the trees!
As the sun rises it looks as if the grass is covered with jewels,
For the dew is melting and the icy crystals are disappearing.
The clouds have wonderful pictures of all things,
You can pretend that they are full of dreams and wishes!
It is as if the spirits in Heaven are helping to raise the sun
And to push all the gloomy clouds away to help clear the sky
For a wonderful, bright, sunny, blue day.
The spring flowers; daffodil, daisy, rose, tulip, buttercup and pansy.
The flowers all play a part in nature, as they sit in my garden day in,
Day out soaking up the sun!
They are so bright, reds, purples, yellows
And the fresh green, green grass.
I love my garden, as the spring approaches all the animals
Come out to play!

Alexandra Angus (12)
Churchmead CE (VA) School

A POEM ABOUT GIRLS AND THEIR FRIENDS

You can go for a pizza and an ice cream too,
You even ask your friends to come with you to the loo,
You can have a night out with them,
You can have a night at home but wherever you will go
You can have a good old moan.

Emily Read (12)
Churchmead CE (VA) School

The Day I Moved House

I'm moving now,
I have nowhere else to go.
As the sun starts setting
I am at home packing away.

I'm moving now,
It's getting darker as I pack.
I walk down those stairs as they're struggling to hold me
And then I think and I remember all the good days in this house.

I'm moving now,
I'm getting closer to the door.
I take one good look around, like a scared tortoise that's
been stepped on,
Then I thought, this will be the last time I'll be standing here.

I'm moving now,
I was being a brave soldier,
I took one deep breath and walked out of the garden.
I ran to the car and opened the door,
As my dad drove, I waved goodbye to my old house.

Amardeep Phagura (12)
Churchmead CE (VA) School

Dreams Will Come True

Dreams will come,
Dreams will go,
Where they take me I do not know.
Out of all the friends I've ever met
You're the one I'll never forget,
If I die before you do,
I'll wait in Heaven just for you.

Dennis Thackeray (12)
Churchmead CE (VA) School

STAR!

In the dark, open sky
Is the glowing star,
If only I could reach that far.
In the distance of the sky
Up above the world so high.
In my eye the star glistens
Like a spy on a mission.
To hold that star has been a dream,
It glows brighter than a beam.
That star shines so bright
In the dark, open sky at night.
Taken by surprise I see
That the star has gone away from me.
It has now become a shooting star,
Gone down the night sky, but is not far.
I make the wish for world peace,
I hope my wish will become true and released.
For I know that I can't reach far
And hold my very own magical star.

Satbir Bhullar (12)
Churchmead CE (VA) School

OCTOBER THOUGHTS

Misty mornings,
Leaves changing colour,
Leaves falling from trees,
Conkers dropping with spiky shells,
Muggy, dark and grey.

Martin Robinson (13)
Churchmead CE (VA) School

MY FIRST DAY AT SCHOOL!

As I walked through the big school gates
I suddenly realised I was with my mates.
I was very nervous, walking slow,
That's because I didn't know where to go.
I was very scared and felt very sad
And I saw some children being bad.
I kept on walking and reached the hall,
It was so big and spacious, it made me feel small.

Later that day I was eating my food
And I wasn't in a happy mood.
I walked outside and was all alone,
This place seemed so far from home.
I waited and waited, time had passed
And as quick as a flash, I was in class.

Slowly and sadly I walked down the steps,
I was positive that science was next.
I found a friend, his name was Kyle
And he always seems to smile.
Now I knew he was quite a good learner,
We started doing work with a Bunsen burner.
Then I had English, the teacher was good
And I saw she was wearing a fleecy hood.
The day was over, I was so relieved.

And I was also very pleased!

Sandeep Bansi (11)
Churchmead CE (VA) School

BABIES

Baby cries in the middle of the night,
Maybe because she had a little fright.

Pick her up,
Give her a feed,
Ah that's better,
That's just what she needs.

In a deep sleep,
Looking very sweet,
She is just perfect,
Small and neat.

Wake up in the morning,
Feeling fine,
She is still asleep at half-past nine.

Then she has a bath,
Nice and clean,
She likes this, does not scream.

Then dress her up into something warm,
Daddy's in the car beeping at the horn.

Out for the day buying something new,
She is not crying, no boo hoo!

Went back home to rest our heads,
She isn't tired so doesn't go to bed.

Louise Welland (13)
Churchmead CE (VA) School

COLOURS!

Blue is the sky,
Cool and dreamy!
Blue is the sea,
Calming and glistening!

Yellow is sunshine,
Beaming through the window!
Yellow is a bumblebee,
Buzzing in the air!

Red is for danger,
Warning everyone!
Red is love,
Heart-warming and caring!

Green is for envy,
Anger, jealousy!
Green is the grass,
Bouncy and soft!

Purple is for royalty,
Stuck up in many ways!
Purple is my room,
Calming as I go to bed!

Rachel Childs (13)
Churchmead CE (VA) School

CONKERS

Conkers fall like thundering rain,
Shells shatter to smithereens,
Greens and browns grind into the ground.

Gaurav Sharma (13)
Churchmead CE (VA) School

THE CREATION OF THE WORLD

The creation of the world had begun,
Light was born and God called it day
While the darkness He kept for night.

God then went on and constructed the Earth,
Created the elements,
The ferocious fire, the strong wind,
The rock-hard land and the strong calm sea.

God then made the fresh green plants,
Grew beauty amongst them,
He watched them as they grew
Through His mighty eyes.

Soon God made the blazing sun
To use to light the day.
He then created the moon and stars
To light up the nightful sky.

God then created birds and fish,
To talk to with excitement
But they would not talk.

God then made His creations talk,
But yet they did not listen.
Later He made humans
To look after His land.

Then God laid and rested,
He thought
And watched His world grow.

James Shoulder (11)
Churchmead CE (VA) School

My Magic Box

(Based on 'The Magic Box' by Kit Wright)

I will put in my box . . .
A sizzling safari shouting silently,
A piano playing with punctuation,
A buffalo begging for a banana.

I will put in my box . . .
One of the teeth from a gigantic bloodthirsty shark,
The sparkling Atlantic Ocean
And the murky marshland,
The last piece of bubbling lava from a scolding volcano.

I will put in my box . . .
A camel in the North Pole
And a polar bear in a desert.

My box is fashioned from . . .
The top of my box is covered in golden Felix feathers,
The hinges of my box are made from the blade of Excaliber,
The inside of my box is covered with T-rex skin.

I will play in my box . . .
I will play with the best millennium
Games there will be.

I will fight in my box . . .
I will fight against all that is evil
With good by my side.

I will surf in my box . . .
I will surf on a sparkling river
Made out of jewels.

Antony Collins (11)
Churchmead CE (VA) School

My First Day

I wanted to get up at the crack of dawn,
To put on a uniform that had never been worn,
I was very excited, could hardly wait
To at last pass through the gate.

At first I felt nervous,
No doubt you'll understand,
All these new surroundings,
Twenty-two acres of land.

When dressed up in my uniform,
It really does feel cool;
I do like the uniform
At this new school.

Many subjects I am fond of,
History could be the best,
The Picts and Scots I've heard about,
Quite soon I'll be taught the rest.

In time I hope to speak good French,
Then use Parlez-vous and other words at home,
Already several words I know,
Which I can practise on the phone.

May I say how much I liked my first day at this school,
I'll always do my best
And never play the fool.

Natalie Thorn (11)
Churchmead CE (VA) School

Rainbow Colours

Yellow's bright,
Yellow's warm,
Yellow's sparkly,
Just like the sun!

Blue is cool,
Blue's refreshing,
Blue like a sapphire,
As blue as the ocean!

Pink is cute,
Pink's sweet,
Pink like a piglet,
Pink as a baby's bottom!

Green is fresh,
Green is everywhere,
Green as the grass,
Green like an apple!

Red is hot,
Red is danger,
Red as a rose,
Red like a flickering flame!

Purple is relaxing,
Purple is calm,
Purple as a violet,
Purple like lavender!

Amy Baker (13)
Churchmead CE (VA) School

My Best Friend Kathryn

She's fun and bubbly,
I think she's lovely.

She's a little bit shy but I don't mind,
When I'm with her we always have a good time.

In my mind she's really outrageous,
But most of the time she's really courageous.

She's always there, even when I'm feeling sad,
Even when I'm happy I still think she's mad.

She's great for going shopping with, she gives me great advice,
What to buy or not to buy, she helps me make up my mind.

She's the best person I've ever met, I think she's great,
I'd never find someone quite as nice as Kathryn, she's my best mate.

Alice Harajda (12)
Churchmead CE (VA) School

The Storm

Lightning flashes through the sky,
The thunder roars out like a lion.
The sky is a grey sheet of paper torn at the edges,
The wind howls like a ghost flying through the sky.
The rain falls from the clouds above,
Gushing through drainpipes and onto the ground,
It knocks on the roof, trying to get in,
Tap, tap, tap.
Coldness fills the atmosphere like a dark blue night's sky.
The sky is dark as if it is about to disappear into nothing.

Craig Andrews (12)
Churchmead CE (VA) School

AUTUMN

The autumn leaves crunched
Like a bag of crisps.
The colours of autumn are
Red like loveable roses,
Yellow like the gleaming sun,
Orange like a flaming fire and
Brown like delicious chocolate.
The air is cold and icy but
Inside's hot and spicy.
All the animals getting ready to hibernate
Look so cute and great.
Summer's gone, autumn's here,
Winter's coming, go on, cheer.

Laura Maunders (12)
Churchmead CE (VA) School

AUTUMN

It's autumn and the leaves are turning red, yellow and brown,
They float slowly to the ground.
The conkers have fallen out of their spiky armoured shells,
The chestnuts are roasting round and round.
The sun is going on holiday and the rain clouds are here again,
The helicopters are spinning around where people have tossed
Them into the air,
The nights are drawing in,
The clocks are winding back,
Hallowe'en is crawling near,
The ghosts and ghouls you can nearly hear.

Emma Philp (12)
Churchmead CE (VA) School

SUNSHINE

(A poem about my cat Stormy)

Stormy, my cat, is a little ray of sunshine,
She is as mad as a hamster in a ball
Going round and round
And as grey as a cloud in a storm.
She rolls on her back on the concrete path
To communicate her joy to the sun!

In the icy days of winter
She is all over me, she gives me puppy-dog eyes,
She wants to sleep on my bed - cupboard love.
She sits huddled in the sun's rays,
Her mind floats on a sunbeam.
She is not a daft cat,
She just loves the gold of her eyes,
They are like the gold of the sun!

Emily Sable (12)
Churchmead CE (VA) School

FIRE!

To start with you were only a tiny flame,
Now you grow and grow.
Your flames set the trees on fire,
Your anger spreads and you glow.
Now you're furious, you're burning,
Destroying wildly.
Then the rain comes,
There's spitting and then a crackle,
Everything's black,
Everything's steaming
And you're gone.

Siân Richards (11)
Churchmead CE (VA) School

THE STORM

I walk home today, it's a sunny day,
The sun was as red as fire,
Drip, drip, drip, drip,
Bang, drip, drip, bang,
I knew I should have caught the bus.
It's a storm,
The hail was hard as rocks,
The lightning was flashing like a camera,
The clouds were crying for everyone.
My house goes knock, knock,
The clouds ran away from the sun
As if they were running for the Olympics.
'What a lovely day.'
'Yes, Mum.'

Vaheed Iqbal (12)
Churchmead CE (VA) School

HANDS OFF

My dad is so kind,
Someone better would be hard to find.
So get your own, you're not having mine,
Just look around and take your time.

My dad is so loving and caring,
Oh yeah and so brave, so daring.
To my mum and me, he's our life,
He vowed to treasure and keep one wife.

So my dad is mine, not yours,
I hope you understand my cause.

Kirsty Dunstan (11)
Churchmead CE (VA) School

Maths

All of the numbers are even or odd,
You'll never confuse them with peas in a pod.
Count with your fingers and count with your toes,
But avoid the highs and stick with the lows.
Some you multiply and some you divide,
Something in you I will confide.
I prefer adding and taking away,
I find that easier any day.
Geometry and algebra are much too confusing,
They're two things I'll not be choosing.
I need a calculator; I can't do without,
With other methods there's always a doubt.
From this poem I guess you can see,
Maths is not the subject for me.
But I will keep trying and become stronger,
For some it is quick, for me it takes longer.

Lucy Hunt (12)
Churchmead CE (VA) School

Blue Is . . .

The birds twittering on a branch, trying to wake the world,
The waves lapping over the soft shore making the sand moist,
The gentle snow lightly covering the mountain tops, melting in the sun,
The bright sky shining over the world, hiding behind,
A carpet of flowers swaying in the strong winds,
The crystals glistening and shining in the blades of grass,
The river flowing, crashing against a rock,
The ink spraying from my pen, making my clothes blue.

Lesha Nair (11)
Churchmead CE (VA) School

My Fat Cat

Long, sleek, black and glossy,
My fat cat Max, lazy but bossy!

He pushes me off the sofa to sleep,
Where he uses his eyes to peep.

He purrs and miaows all contented
And sleeps on the sofa, soft and dented!

Sometimes Max roams the street
In the dead of night when we're all asleep.

He hunts for mice and picks a fight
With other cats out at night.

I think I would like to be a cat
With a lazy life, just fancy that!

Stephanie Brain (11)
Churchmead CE (VA) School

A Storm

The boat was rushing over the sea,
Like a fight for freedom.
The sounds of crushing leaves is
The sound of a newspaper being turned.
The tops of houses fly off,
As the angry wind swallows them in one gulp.
The flash of lightning groaning,
As it leapt out of the sky.
The sea looked as if he was
Opening his mouth and swallowing the boat
As it disappeared behind the wave.

Kirsty Williamson (12)
Churchmead CE (VA) School

The Beach

Sapphire sea
Scorching sun
Golden sand . . .
The sun sparkles in the sea,
As ice creams melt slowly
Like snow in the palm of your hand,
Children play,
Adults sunbathe,
As darkness approaches,
People leave,
Wind howls
Like a wolf in the woods,
Rocks cry
Like a baby hungrily waiting,
Waves viciously splash against the shoreline,
Now it's silent,
The beach is empty.

Zara Hussain (13)
Churchmead CE (VA) School

My Rabbit

My rabbit is as fluffy as a bunny,
Always wanting to get out of its hutch.
Scratching, scrapping,
Moaning, groaning,
Eating, sleeping,
Hopping, bopping,
Protesting not to go back,
That's my rabbit, good old Floppy!

Sukhmonique Dosanjh (11)
Churchmead CE (VA) School

WINTER

I remember,
One morning in December,
I awoke to the sound of silence.
I was warm in bed,
As I poked out my head,
Out from under the cover.
I peeked through a gap in the curtain
And I had to check to be certain,
That I was not dreaming.
The trees looked like scales,
Balancing the weight of snow,
The leafless branches cradle the robin,
For he has nowhere else to go.

Kathryn Butcher (12)
Churchmead CE (VA) School

FORGOT IT AT SECONDARY SCHOOL

Forgot it at secondary school,
RE homework!
Forgot it at secondary school,
Materials for textiles!
Forgot it at secondary school,
Eleven pages of maths!
Forgot it at secondary school,
PE kit!
Forgot it at secondary school,
Ingredients for cooking!

I've got another detention!

Michael Higgs (11)
Churchmead CE (VA) School

First Day Nerves

Time to get up,
Still tired, it's too early.
I wash and eat,
No time to stop,
Keep checking the clock.

Nervous, off I go,
Mum drops me off at school.
Look for my friends
And go to the school hall.

Thinking of my old school,
It made me feel sad,
But at the end of the day
My new school was not that bad.

Adrian Burn (10)
Churchmead CE (VA) School

King Of The Ring

I wake up on Saturday at quarter to nine,
To be ready to watch a programme which is mighty fine.
The characters you meet are bulky, big and tall,
But some of them are known to be a bit small.
They use props like tables and chairs
And they've got to make sure that the referee is unaware.
Their music is unique and is always bone-crushing,
Like the spines of people's bodies constantly bashing.
But one stands in front of all,
He is the mighty one,
He is the legend,
He is the one who eliminates them all.

Pavendeep Bansel (11)
Churchmead CE (VA) School

LONELY SOUL

There was a girl in London
Who walked the streets every day,
She had no home to go to
Nor a bed in which to lay!

She walked bare-footed on the streets
In rags covered with dirt and mud,
Without the rags, the mud, the dirt
She would be beautiful like a bud!

She did not have a lover
Until one day he came,
He picked her up from the gutter,
He did not give a name!

She was no longer a poor girl,
But a very, very rich one.
She had a very good name
And had gold by the tonne!

When her lover died
She lost all her riches,
Became a poor girl again
And slept in the ditches!

Rachel Bruce (13)
Churchmead CE (VA) School

COLOURS

Red is a heart, a broken heart,
Blue is the ocean crashing the rocks,
Green is the grass where the bugs crawl
And pink is the colour of a woman's shawl.

Grey is a storm with lightning that lights the sky,
Black is the night where the babies cry,
White is the clouds which are like patches of paint
And yellow is the sun which flies over the neighbour's gate.

Leah Smith (11)
Churchmead CE (VA) School

READY FOR SCHOOL

New blazer and shirts,
New trousers and skirts,
New black polished shoes,
My clean pressed shirt
With my tie too tight,
With my bag full to the brim,
Too heavy to carry
I sling on my back,
What shall I do with this heavy backpack?

All ready for school,
All bright and alert,
What will I learn?
Will I take it all in?
How can I concentrate with all this din?

Can't wait for lunch,
Not long to go now.
Last lesson is over,
Ready to go home.

Maybe I'll give Mum a ring, on my way home.

Lauren O'Brien (11)
Churchmead CE (VA) School

PRISON

Society is the prison
People are the jury
Tears are the pain
Scars are the marks
Enemies are the cell mates
Houses are the cells
Friends are the visitors
Skin is the uniform
Politics are the guards
Presidents are the inspectors
Kings and queens are the judges
Schools are the courts
Lessons are the court sessions
Walls are the bars
Food is the poison
Life is the sentence
Death is the only freedom.

Nathan Lee (13)
Churchmead CE (VA) School

THE SAND, SEA AND SUN

On the golden sand is where I stand
With an ice cream melting in my hand.

In the deep blue sea is where I swim,
Hardly able to stand.

The red-hot sun high in the sky,
Watching, waiting for a seagull to fly.

On the golden sand is where I stand
With an ice cream melting in my hand.

Khuliswa Khwela-Browning (11)
Churchmead CE (VA) School

Winter Is Nearly Here

There's a nip in the air,
The days are getting shorter,
Darkness descends earlier and earlier as the days go by.
The leaves on the trees are changing colour,
Gold, bronze, red and brown,
Falling off the branches to the ground.
The wind awakens and begins to tremble
As it gathers up speed and disturbs nature's calm.
The sky becomes overcast,
Grey, gloomy and dull.
The rain falls, gently at first,
Then harder and harder, vigorously
Beating down, pounding the earth,
Then all is quiet,
There's a nip in the air,
Winter is nearly here.

Rachel Davies (11)
Churchmead CE (VA) School

My First Day

On my first day at school
I was nervous,
I was suspicious,
At lunch the chips were delicious.

On my first day at school
I didn't know where to go.
I got lost,
I had my lunch, but didn't know how much it cost.

That was my first day!

Navrupe Bachra (11)
Churchmead CE (VA) School

My School Week!

On my first day at school . . .
My twin embarrassed me.
On my first day at school . . .
I learn schoolology.

On my second day at school . . .
My sister wouldn't come.
On my second day at school . . .
She was dragged there by my mum.

On my third day at school . . .
I explored everywhere.
On my third day at school . . .
I fell off my chair.

On my fourth day at school . . .
My teacher got stuck in red tape.
On my fourth day at school . . .
Me and my twin escaped.

My school week!

Rupy Bachra
Churchmead CE (VA) School

October Thoughts

Cold winter night,
Brown leaves fall from branches,
Trees die like old people.

Henry Wenman (13)
Churchmead CE (VA) School

PUPPIES

Puppies, puppies,
What should I call my puppy?
Rex, Bobby, Oscar, Benji or even Ponce?
I just don't know what to call him.

He is really lovely.
I hold him ever so tight
And I cuddle him all through the night.

He likes playing in big black sacks
And he especially likes sleeping on my back.
When I get home, I get out his comb and brush him.
He loves it so much he rolls on his back
And then he will sit on the soft mat.

Then I found the name for him,
I called him Happy because you see,
He's always wagging his tail at me.

Victoria Green (11)
Churchmead CE (VA) School

MY DUCKS

I got my ducks when they were three weeks old,
They hardly had any feathers so they were cold.
They are getting bigger and stronger by the week
And they are now on their feet.
We made them a wooden pen,
I think they'll like their new den.
Jemima might lay eggs next year,
I really love having them here.

Georgina Dunford (12)
Churchmead CE (VA) School

All Alone!

All alone
In a house
There was a boy
And his mouse.

His mouse was little,
He was too.
He was so young
And needed the loo.

By himself
His mum was gone.
He was so bored
And she was so long.

He was hungry,
His name was Murry
So he made himself
A little curry.

Inderpreet Dhanda (13)
Churchmead CE (VA) School

Light

The flame shining oh so bright,
Blinding me like a flashing torch light.
Glaring, shielding all my sight,
I can see no more
Emptiness,
So blank,
Nothing to live for.

Natalie Everett (11)
Churchmead CE (VA) School

Double, Double, Toil And Trouble

Double, double, toil and trouble,
Mixed up skin, water bubbles.
Badgers and moles digging holes,
Eating up dirty coals.

Ice cream mixed about,
Trying to say, 'Let me out.'
Bits of toes, ears of teddy bears,
Cut up clothes, filthy underwear.

Gingerbread men playing tag,
Trying to find a girl with a bag.
Double, double, toil and trouble,
Boiling hot, water bubbles.

Tara Kang (11)
Churchmead CE (VA) School

My Shadow

My shadow's dim and sunless,
Whatever I do it does,
But as soon as night falls
My shadow disappears.
As soon as it's morning
I see it yet again,
Shadows are unmakeable
Without the sun and light.
My shadow is always behind me,
It'll never go away
Unless I stand right under the sun,
Then my shadow will be gone.

Laura-Ann Hearn (11)
Churchmead CE (VA) School

DRAGONS

Dragons, fire-breathing monsters with long rippling tails,
And gleaming scales reflecting the sun's rays.

Dragons, fire-breathing monsters with sly,
Glaring eyes and sharp, shredding claws.

Dragons, fire-breathing monsters with bat-shaped wings and their curved snouts,
With smoke seeping through their nostrils and into the air around.

Dragons, fire-breathing monsters with jaws
Full of pointed teeth and their short, stumpy legs.

Dragons are mythical creatures but are very beautiful
Because of their rainbow-coloured bodies.

Victoria Crawley (11)
Churchmead CE (VA) School

CURRY

Add on spice,
Boil some rice,
Two-meal course
With some sauce,
Finger-licking tandoori chicken,
Taste buds kicking,
Lamb balti,
A little salty,
Don't hurry,
Enjoy your curry.

Liam Gorman (13)
Churchmead CE (VA) School

THE STORY OF THE LONELY HIPPO

There stands a hippo
All alone,
Grunting and yawning
On his own.

But alone no more
As you will see,
A mate comes by
They're as happy as can be.

So there they stand,
Quite tall and grand.
They're quite a sight
In the sunset's light.

Laura Turner (11)
Churchmead CE (VA) School

MY HOLIDAY

The sun was blazing
And the beach was amazing.
The food was lovely
And the sea was warm and bubbly.
Every day I swam in the pool
Because the water was fresh and cool.
Everyone was happy and kind,
I really enjoyed the treasure find.
The sand was soft and gold
But alas . . . now I'm home the weather is wet and cold.

Marcus Tongue (12)
Churchmead CE (VA) School

As He Stares At Us

So our teacher says
As he stares at us,
As he glares at us,
Get a move,
Sit down and shut up,
Use your brain,
Chop, chop,
Stop moaning.

So our teacher says
As he stares at us,
As he glares at us,
We haven't got all day,
Sometime this year would be nice,
You can do better than that,
Where's your homework,
You've got a half an hour detention.

So our teacher says,
As he stares at us,
As he glares at us,
That work should be finished,
Where are your manners?
Who do you think you are?
That is much too messy,
That work is not acceptable.

That is all we hear.

Danielle Kempton (12)
Churchmead CE (VA) School

SUMMER HAS GONE, AUTUMN IS HERE

S ummer has gone,
U ntil this day,
M any leaves have fallen,
M ost leaves are still on the trees,
E very day comes, goes, more leaves on the floor,
R ain has come once again.

H as summer gone for good?
A utumn is here,
S ummer has gone.

G one for good,
O nce more summer has gone,
N early all leaves are off the trees,
E very day autumn is here.

A round this world summer has disappeared,
U ntil this day,
T rees have no leaves,
U ntil this day,
M any leaves are on the floor,
N ow that autumn is here.

I n this autumn day,
S hivering people shall come.

H ere autumn is,
E very day comes, goes, more leaves on the floor,
R ain is here too,
E very day, autumn is here.

Kirstie Banks (12)
Churchmead CE (VA) School

My Name Is Khadija Baker

My name is Khadija Baker
I can be a troublemaker.
Every day I play a trick,
People say I take the mick.

I run around going mad,
People say I'm very bad.
Every week I get a detention,
I do it all just to get attention!

I scream and shout
Whilst running about.
I push in line
Every lunchtime.

I chat through classes
And take the mick out of people wearing glasses.
They tell me off for no reason,
But they always say I tease them.
This is because I get over-excited
But that is because I'm a different kid!

Khadija Baker (11)
Churchmead CE (VA) School

Liverpool

Liverpool, Liverpool are the best,
Better than all the rest.
Owen is the one who makes the game,
Talented, skilful, with lots of fame.

Kyle Igbinidion (11)
Churchmead CE (VA) School

SPELL

Hubble, bubble
Let's make some trouble!

I shall throw in;
A frog in a box,
A bat in a hat,
A sweet, crackle, pop and fancy that.

How about something else;
Some wind, not a twister,
An eagle's beak, yep that sounds right
To eat and one more thing,
A screech from a girl!
Just right.

Hubble, bubble
I've made some trouble!

Now you know not to mess with the witch of the east,
Otherwise you'll be turned into a beast.

This is the end of the trouble spell,
Unless you prefer to be turned into a bell.
Ding-a-ling-a-ling!

Mercedes Caulton (11)
Churchmead CE (VA) School

OCTOBER

Yellow leaves drop like rain in a storm,
Skies dull like steamed up windows,
The sun sinks like a stone in water.

Stephen Parkins (13)
Churchmead CE (VA) School

IN MY BOX

In my box
There's a newborn puppy drinking from its mother.
There's the first twinkle from a baby's eye.

In my box
There's the first word from a bumblebee
And the first buzz from a human.

My box is
Covered with diamonds and stars
And it's got wishes in its corners,
With a dolphin handle.

I went skiing in my box
To Mount Everest,
My hair was flying everywhere.

Sonya Jalif (11)
Churchmead CE (VA) School

HAMSTER, HAMSTER

Hamster, hamster eyes so bright.
Hamster, hamster comes out at night.
Hamster, hamster big wet nose.
Hamster, hamster and his tiny toes.
Hamster, hamster furry and beige.
Hamster, hamster in your cage.
If you're ill you'll see my tears
Because I want to love you for years and years.

Michaela Hamblin (11)
Churchmead CE (VA) School

I Was Once A Baby

I was once a baby,
Cute as can be.
I was once a baby,
Everyone loved me.

I grew up with my family,
Everywhere I went they followed me.
I grew up with my family,
They helped when I bruised my knee.

Now I'm getting older by the day,
Going to school and having fun.
Now I'm getting older by the day,
Older in the past, then and now - today.

Kelly Chivers (12)
Churchmead CE (VA) School

Theme Parks

Roller coasters everywhere,
In everyone's eyes there is a tear.
Merry-go-round I hate so much,
I won't even dare to touch!

Babies look at you and cry,
You sit on rides, they start to fly.
Theme parks, enjoyable places,
Where you see happy faces!

Wasil Akhtak (11)
Churchmead CE (VA) School

The Magic Box

(Based on 'The Magic Box' by Kit Wright)

I will put in my box . . .
The white dress from the first wedding of the year,
The gold bangle from a baby's christening,
A baby's first word.

I will put in my box . . .
The golden rings from around Saturn,
The red-hot sun from Mars,
The silver moon from Jupiter.

I will put in my box . . .
The sound of my friends playing,
The sound of people crying,
The sound of happy children.

My box is full of happiness,
My box is full of kindness,
My box is full of things about me.

Sainie Hobdell (11)
Churchmead CE (VA) School

Blue Is . . .

A flash of lightning piercing through the night sky,
The shadow under the eyes of an innocent newborn baby,
A fish relaxing in a calm lake,
A glittering crystal shining like a star in the timeless sky,
The flames of a candle lighting up the dark room,
Chelsea kicking their way through the match,
Italy facing another football match.

Harleen Grewal (11)
Churchmead CE (VA) School

AUTUMN CHANGES

Autumn is a time of many changes,
Leaves they turn from green to brown
And then they all fall down.

The morning grass is covered with dew,
Daylight hours they are so few.

The leaves go crunch as you walk,
Your breath goes white as you talk.

As harvest comes the fruits go ripe,
There are fruits being picked of every type.

As the days are shorter we get an extra hour in bed,
The trees go to sleep and the flowers are dead.

Squirrels and hedgehogs sleep winter through
While blue tits and robins sing as they do.

Sarah Margetts (11)
Churchmead CE (VA) School

STARS!

When the stars come out at night-time
While the moon is shining bright,
The only bird awake
Is the owl that hoots all night.

When you look at the stars at night
Do you wonder at what you see?
Is it diamonds or jewels that twinkle in the sky?
What do you think stars could be?

Calella Ward (11)
Churchmead CE (VA) School

It's Unfair

Day in, day out
I hear this whinging and whining,
Why?
It's like a non-stop record
Over and over again.

Help! It's annoying,
My sister says it,
My brother says it,
I'm starting to say it.

I'm not like that, to whinge or whine,
But I'm addicted to saying,
It's unfair!

Siân Heatman (11)
Churchmead CE (VA) School

My Favourite Cat

My lovely pet Tom is a cat,
He is funny and fat.
He likes sitting and curling up on my lap
But he often sleeps on a mat.

He is sometimes sad and sometimes mad,
He always purrs when he sees my dad.
He jumps up when he sees my nan
But I'm his favourite fan.

Vicky Clements (11)
Churchmead CE (VA) School

There Was A . . .

There was a huge dog who chewed his favourite log,
There was a small kitten who always liked to sob,
There was a long worm who liked to wiggle,
There was a plump pig who always liked to giggle,
There was a big dinner lady who always liked to serve,
There was a roof with one big curve.
There was my good ending
But I'm sending it to you.

Sati Nandra (11)
Churchmead CE (VA) School

He's Not My Whole Life But He Makes My Life Whole

His eyes are as big as dinner plates,
His feet are like Wellington boots,
My dad's lost his place on the sofa
And curses at the hairs on his suits.

My puppy dog's tummy's expanding,
As well as his choice in socks,
My sister and brother's toys are decreasing,
He's cheekier than a fox.

The slightest touch of his lead and by magic . . . he appears
And the rattle of a can or the squeak of a cupboard . . . he hears,
Yet, it's curious that on walks he's completely deaf
And my calls I'm sure . . . he fears,
For he knows at the end that the lead means home . . .
And he's got other ideas!

Emma Settle (11)
Claires Court Girls' College

This Mysterious Thing

When I caught one this morning
I didn't know what to do.
But then I found the solution
And now I'm telling you.

I let it take over my face,
It spread from ear to ear.
I got extremely happy,
No longer did I feel fear.

I heard some people talking,
I saw some people stare.
I wondered what they wanted,
Maybe I didn't brush my hair.

Maybe I looked stupid,
But no one wanted to say.
Maybe I looked great,
I wondered either way.

That was when I realised,
I could feel it went for a mile.
I'll tell you what this thing was,
I'll tell you it was a smile!

Naomi Thomas (12)
Claires Court Girls' College

LIFE'S AGES

Like Mother Nature's shifting seasons,
Imagine how our life does change.
A bud will form and then will wither,
From birth till death is our great range.

Imagine life at its dawning,
The smells of sunrise, soft, pink, blue.
Sprouting, budding, stretching, yawning,
Fresh spring sounds emerge anew.

Imagine colour bursting boldly,
Youthful mood of heat and rage.
Contrasting greens to cool the anger,
Reflecting nature's lively age.

Imagine freshly ripened apples,
Maturely round, red and gold.
Tossing, tumbling, leaves are falling,
Dusk is calling in the cold.

Imagine nature's heart is sleeping,
Buried deep beneath the earth.
Crisp white snow upon its surface,
Blankets the hope of its rebirth.

Sophie Denney (12)
Claires Court Girls' College

PUPPY

Naughty puppy chasing your tail,
Stop it right now you're causing a gale.
Twisting and turning you're getting so scruffy,
What happened to my cute fluffy puppy?

You chew up my socks instead of your ball,
But you do come along every time I call.
Wagging your tail you look so happy,
Come play with me sweet little chappy.

Your eyes so so big and coat is so white,
You're the most loveable thing in sight.
With eyes like buttons and a little pink tongue,
I knew straight away that you were the one.

The first day I got you I was so very lucky,
Because you're an adorable sweet little puppy.
I know we will stay together forever,
Come rain or shine, whatever the weather!

Jordan Lewis (11)
Claires Court Girls' College

LYING IN WAIT . . .

Wait, look at that light,
in the middle of the night,
the woman walks and disappears,
he follows her and round he peers.

He hears some talking
and some walking,
then some violence
and suddenly silence.

She is coming back oh yes, oh yes,
in that ugly old black dress,
he pounces on her like a cat.
Oh drat, oh drat, she got away
in the silence of the day.

Elissa Field (11)
Claires Court Girls' College

Walking In The Rain

She does not walk very fast but she doesn't move too slow,
Her way of movement is gentle but not swift.
Her raincoat's tight, the flowers are a bit dull as the rain drips off,
But her feet keep padding along like there's a rhythm inside.
The umbrella is blowing in and out,
The rain is going pitter-patter, drip, drop but she keeps walking,
Her tender hands hold her shopping bags firm
And steady in the wet weather.
Her spotty hat holds her hair down as a lazy wind begins to form
But her steady feet keep going.
Her soft, warm face smiles meekly at pedestrians hurriedly passing,
No one stops to help, no one stops to say hello
As her soft lipstick wears gradually away.
The lines on her face are faint but show a nice side to her,
The way she smiles in a warm and welcoming way.
Her eyes are a baby blue with a kindness behind them
And her face is thoughtful and quiet with a deep expression
That shows you the generosity inside.
She smells like peppermint creams, which are always in her handbag.
No one can see the things inside which shine out,
No one looks properly to see the goodness inside
But no matter what she keeps on walking in the rain . . .

Nicole Hogan (12)
Claires Court Girls' College

In This Hand A Pen I Take

In this hand a pen I take
But no writing I do make
But a single word of loneliness.

In this hand your hand I take
But no movement do I make
But a single word of friendship.

In his hand a rose I take
But no speaking do I make
But a single word of love.

Imogen Brain (11)
Claires Court Girls' College

My Mum

My mum is a . . .

Long talker
Loud sleeper
Food cooker
Tea drinker
Friend maker
Great ironer
Flower lover
School helper
Clothes shopper
Dish washer
Chocolate eater
And a great mother.

Nathan Clarke (11)
Easthampstead Park School

The Haunted House

You never see it,
All you hear is the creaky floorboards,
Sounds like a small scurrying mouse,
Stands there and watches you,
Creaking the floorboards
Like a small scurrying mouse,
It is the fear of the house,
As you go up the stairs you
Round every corner as you
Walk with fear,
And look behind you . . .
You might just see it!

Andrew Rawlins (11)
Easthampstead Park School

My Niece

Big hugger
Cute toddler
Tweenies watcher
Toy bringer
Tricycle rider
Juice drinker
Messy drawer
Ice cream eater
Auntie lover!

Serina Haynes (11)
Easthampstead Park School

I'M STILL ON YOUR SIDE

(Dedicated to my little brother with love always)

Hush now; wipe away your tears,
I'm still on your side,
Always have been, that isn't about to change,
Even when life seems tough and crashes down,
Any time, day or night,
I'm still on your side.

Don't you sigh, everything will be okay,
I'm still on your side,
When the others let you down,
Life begins to look rough
And think you can't take any more,
Remember that I'm still on your side.

When it seems the whole world has turned against you,
I'm still on your side,
Things get rough and things get tough,
Everything seems to be turning upside down,
Confused you stumble on,
Let me show you the way, I'm still on your side.

I'll be there when you need me,
I won't let you down,
There isn't anything I wouldn't do for you.
I'll give you strength when you need it,
A shoulder for your tears,
A helping hand through difficult times
And I'll always remember your smile,
There is always sun after the rain . . .
I'm still on your side.

Jayne Ellmes (16)
Easthampstead Park School

The Salty Sea

Salty sea
Punching people
Under umbrellas
Blue balls
Fish feet
Bouncing birds
Drunk donkeys
Soft sand
Sun surfing.

Laura Lovett (11)
Easthampstead Park School

Autumn

As autumn gets closer the weather gets colder
And leaves are all around.
They're red, yellow, gold and brown
And scatter themselves on the ground.
Trees look bare, empty and plain.
In spring the leaves they'll all grow back again.

Lots of pumpkins are being seen.
As it gets close to Hallowe'en,
Lots of children all dress up,
Lipstick, costumes and make-up.

November the 5th fireworks are here,
Cats and dogs stay in with fear.
Fireworks zoom through the sky,
Soaring free, soaring high.

Autumn comes just once a year,
Followed by some Christmas cheer.

Carla Benn (11)
Hemdean House School

A Poem For Mum

I love my mum,
Full of cuddles and kindness.
She says I'm a star
But really she is, a star in the sky.

When she tucks me in,
She hugs me tight,
She says I'll never be alone,
That I'm always safe, in her arms.

Wherever I am,
I'm only safe,
When I'm with her.

I can't explain
How close we are,
She is my
Shining star.

I love her to the moon and back,
I'd love her for eternity.
Even if I was paid all the money in the world,
I would still want her next to me.

Annie Fawke (11)
Hemdean House School

Winter Poem

Snow falls on the ground
And covers all around.
Boys sledge down the snowy road,
The sledge holds their heavy load.

The ice is very cold and white
Which gives me frostbite.
It's hard to go on without skates,
We might just run into one of our mates.

Snowman standing still
On an ice-cold hill.
He's wearing a scarf,
It's funny, it makes me laugh.

Katie-Louise Smith (11)
Hemdean House School

Hallowe'en

There is a pumpkin,
Shining bright,
Inside the pumpkin, candlelight.
It must be Hallowe'en tonight!
The giant goblin woke up,
Rushed to the party site.
I saw a witch go riding high,
On her broomstick through the sky.
The aliens peeping through the gates,
They also want to celebrate.
The Devil is watching little kids,
As they run through, trick or treat.
I saw a pixie,
Small and fine,
He was jumping on the washing line.
The witch's cat Malisa Brown,
Turned the church clock upside down.
The tooth fairy sparkling in the sky
And showing off
I don't know why.
The friendly ghost came along
And sang a cheerful party song.
So don't miss out on the fun tonight
And celebrate the Hallowe'en night.

Fatima Adalbaeva (13)
Hemdean House School

Sakura

One by one they bloom
Into delicate pink hues
All over the land.

Twisted and gnarled trees
Burst into cherry blossom
Spreading their pink snow.

Beautiful blossom
Falls silently to the ground
As a breeze glides by.

One by one they fade
The pink Sakura blossom . . .
The plant of Japan.

Sarah-Jayne Harris (11)
Hemdean House School

Beneath The Sea Foam

Beneath the sea foam dolphins glide
Swishing around the low and high tides.

Beneath the sea foam fishes dodge
While the octopus squirts out misty splodge.

Beneath the sea foam sea horses prance
And the startling starfish wave and dance.

Beneath the sea foam is a nice place to be
Peacefully in the shiny sea!

Megan Campbell (11)
Hemdean House School

SEASONS HAIKUS

Autumn
Leaves fall in autumn:
And a kitten comes to play
Rolling in dried leaves.

Summer
Sunset in summer:
Bees in their striped pyjamas
Flying to their beds.

Winter
Snowflakes in winter:
Polar bears in white, warm coats
Play fight all day long.

Spring
Wind blows in springtime:
The treetops dance in the breeze
So elegantly.

Anna Harries & Estelle Birch (11)
Hemdean House School

AUTUMN DAYS

Leaves, fall,
Sun's gone,
Sky's grey,
No fun!
It's cold and damp,
Miserable and wet,
Autumn's the time
We never forget.

Marika Skeete (11)
Hemdean House School

My Burmese Cat

My Burmese,
Is always trying to please,
Always in a muddle,
Wanting a big cuddle,
His eyes are yellow,
He's such a friendly fellow,
He loves a tummy tickle,
When he gets into a pickle,
I adore his loud purr,
His shiny, soft fur,
He has a special toy,
My little chocolate boy,
He hides his mouse,
All around the house,
He has a special name,
I call him simply, James,
I love my Burmese,
Who is always trying to please,
He is never very far,
My mainman, moviestar!

Helen Rudd (11)
Hemdean House School

Teddy Bear

Teddy bear is always there,
Big, round eyes full of surprise,
He's so sweet with honey fur.
Special clothes, glasses for his nose,
Soft and cuddly, oh how lovely!

Alexandra Wells (11)
Hemdean House School

My Wish

(For my mum)

Love is a special thing,
Your hopes, dreams and wishes
In all your heart.
All I need is you through everything,
All the time I wish you would be
Here with me.
In my heart, by my side.

Harland Dewar (11)
Hemdean House School

Goodbye Mrs Wright

As I started on the first day,
Every little kid shouted, 'Hip, hip, hooray!'
But I don't want to leave my mum and dad,
But maybe this won't be quite so bad.

As I started school quite late in the year,
Maybe I shouldn't go to this school, not here.
I walked through the door, the kids looked around,
They all cheered, but I didn't make a sound.

I walked further towards my chair,
The teacher didn't look like a big, growly bear.
'Who will take care of this little girl?'
A girl turned round with a head like a pearl.

I went up the school, older and older,
I look bright, happy, cheery and bolder.
It was time to finish school, but not quite,
So I went to year 1 and said goodbye to Mrs Wright.

Victoria Richmond-Bowell (11)
Highdown School

The New School

Tick-tock, tick-tock,
The clock never seems to stop,
Brrr . . . it finally goes,
Next lesson, next lesson,
Where is it?
Lost, lost,
Other kids pushing into you,
Teacher shouting.

Finally the next lesson appears,
Time to face up to all my fears,
Thoughts running through my mind,
Detentions, homework,
Bullies, strict teachers,
Brrr . . . the clock goes again,
Time for lunch,
The line.

The line, the huge long line of older kids in a queue,
Waiting to get to the front.
Ugh, disgusting! This food is disgusting.
No lunch, now for last lesson,
The long corridors, scary kids,
English, writing in pen, forever writing in pen.
Out of the lesson, home time.

Catching the bus home,
Loads of things being thrown,
The bus driver staying calm,
Dancing, diving, missing the lot,
Loads of kids get off.
The only kid on the bus,
Finally, nearly home.

Off the bus I run,
Trying to get home to have some fun.
Safe at home,
Warm and safe,
But tomorrow it happens all over again.

Kathryn Harris (11)
Highdown School

FIRST DAY OF SCHOOL

F ighting my way to dinner
I s this where I'm supposed to be?
R eally not being a winner!
S hall I go home, we'll see.
T here goes the bell.

D o I go to class
A n unusual smell!
Y ou should go fast.

A nd where do I go?
T ime to go!

S o many lessons!
C ool I say!
H elp I'm lost!
O ut of the door comes the sea
O f students after the bell.
L ater I go home.
'I had a nice day at school.'
(That's what I told my mum at least).

Robert Piper (11)
Highdown School

My Primary Memory Poem

F rightening people!
I solated!
R ough children,
S trangers to me,
T easers.

D oors not open,
A ges different,
Y oung people,

O ld people,
F resh start!

S urrounded by giants,
C riticising kids,
H ated school,
O n my own.
O rganised, I wasn't but other people were!
L aughter, evil laughter!

Liam Newens (11)
Highdown School

First Day At Secondary School

6th September, first day of school,
Frightened, scared, acting like a fool.
Pretending to be asleep, pretending to be sick,
My mum won't fall for all my tricks.
I put on my uniform, feeling rather nauseous,
I walk to school being very cautious.
I get to school and there are my mates,
Till this day I've had no lates.

Scott Walker (11)
Highdown School

First Day

First day,
Scary isn't it?
Everyone's bigger than you.
Sends shivers down your spine.
Moving between lessons is bad enough,
But actually having new lessons and subjects,
That's even worse.

First day,
Secondary school, it's massive,
Which building am I supposed to be in?
This one?
That one? Who knows.
I'm late for my lesson,
Worried I'll get a DT.

First day,
New teachers.
Strict ones, nice ones,
But they all give you homework
And lots of it.
I think, will I have friends,
Will I be a loner
Or will I be the most popular in the form?

First day,
Everyone has it,
Everyone goes through it,
But the first days are the worst,
That's for sure.

Claire Munnings (11)
Highdown School

EMMER GREEN TRAGEDY

Clinging, clinging,
'Please don't let me leave here!
Please stay with me.
I'm scared, everything's so big.'

Sobbing, sobbing,
'We have to go!'
'Let me come with you!'
'You can't come with us!
But we can stay a little longer.'

A little longer came.
'We really have to go now.'
'Why?'
The teacher freed my parents
They started to go
'No! Mummy! Daddy!'

I started to calm down
Or so the teacher said.
'Now can any of you spell your name?'
'I can,' I whispered.

Finally a bell rang and I rushed out.
'Glad I'm see you to!'
'You mean: I'm glad to see you!'
'That's what I said!'

'How was your day?'
'Great! Can I go again tomorrow?'
'Of course you can!' they laughed.
'What's so funny!'

Claire Crew (12)
Highdown School

HIGHDOWN

H is for hurry up, you're going to be late!
I is for all the interesting subjects
G is for gain all the different rewards
H is for history, oh so boring!
D is for dinner hall, *I'm hungry*
O is for oh my God! I'm finally here
W is for worries, *I've left my book at home*
N is for nervous, exactly what I am.

S is for science and a Bunsen burner
C is for my class with all my friends
H is for home that's where I'm going
O is for open my pencil case
O is for I'm out of here!
L is for listen there's the bell,
Ring! Ring!

Samuel Kelsal (11)
Highdown School

PRIMARY SCHOOL: THE FIRST DAY

S cary people everywhere
C ounting is too hard for me
H ow am I ever going to get past all the pushing people?
O nly me, I've lost my class on the way to assembly
'O kay,' said the teacher, 'sit down, let's read a story.'
L ong have I waited to go home to my mum.

Rebecca White (11)
Highdown School

First Day Of Primary School

Enter the doors, big doors,
(Why do they have handles so high you can't reach them?)
Walk down the hall
Meet a big, tall lady: she shows me to class
(Where is class?)
The corridor's so long you could get lost.

I'm in, into the class
Where lots of unfriendly devils sit and stare
(At me? Who knows!)
Then, *brrriiinnnggg!* What's that?
Where's everyone going?
(I think I'll follow them)

The playground's so big, you could get lost
(I won't!)
I go round a corner
Look!
A fan thingy
Wait this place doesn't look familiar.
Hey, where am I?
Help! I'm *lost!*

Christopher Mollett (11)
Highdown School

First Day At School

My brand new uniform on,
My heavy bag on my back,
A long walk up the hill to school,
My stomach quivering as I go.

Entering the spacious barn,
I get shown to my seat,
Listen to Mrs Wilson's long welcome speech.

Next we're sent with our tutor,
Into our tutor rooms,
Another new teacher calls out loads of names,
Some I know, but others I don't.
After that we go outside for a school quiz.
The stairs, they are so big here, some pupils too,
But we are just new.

Rebecca Hill (11)
Highdown School

My First Day At School

Mum!
Is this school?
So where's the swimming pool?
I walked up to the gate,
Mum looked at her watch,
Oh no you're late!
I started to walk in,
I walked straight into a bin,
I looked at the fish
And made a wish,
That I was back home in bed.
I opened my eyes
And to my surprise,
I was standing in the middle of a field.
Then a lady came out
And started to shout,
Suddenly I was in a classroom,
I am doomed.
The day slowly drew to an end,
Oh can I do this again?

Tuesday Holder (11)
Highdown School

My First Day At Highdown

I was walking down the long, narrow road,
Behind big children,
Children older than me,
Scary children.
I look behind me again,
This time at my mum,
Getting smaller and smaller,
Until she was gone,
Disappeared, vanished.

A lady told me to go to the dinner hall,
The dinner hall?
I looked this way and that for the dinner hall,
I decided to follow everybody else,
It seemed like I was walking for hours,
Until I finally found it.

A big, tall man,
With blacky-grey hair
And a little beard,
Came over to me and asked me
To sit next to this boy at the back.
He was smaller than me,
But I think he was older,
He wasn't so scary.

At the end of the day there was my mum,
A smile on her face
And a smile on mine.

Samantha Fisher (11)
Highdown School

First Day

Six miles, I thought,
At least six miles.
Six whole miles away from home.
I don't think I've been that far
Away from home before.

My first task was to find the tutor.
I thought (and I still do)
That a tutor was a teacher
Who taught you at home
My brother had one.

I'm hungry!
What is the point in this
Never-ending queue?
All my time at Highdown
Will be spent waiting in this endless queue.

What?
Five pieces of homework a day?
I had homework at primary school
But not as much as this.

'What's the union of A and B times the square root
Of seventy-four equally divided by the factor of six?'
My maths teacher bellowed at the class of empty heads
And emotionless faces.

Duncan Cornee (11)
Highdown School

SECONDARY SCHOOL

It's so big, like a maze,
I run up and down confused,
I look around, so many ways,
I just don't know where to go.

There are doors everywhere,
All these corridors perplex me,
Is maths up this stair?
I really just can't cope!

Oh help I'm lost!
I'll be late
And how much does dinner cost?
I don't think I've got enough!
What's on the menu?
Oh no, I've forgotten half my stuff!
Wonder who's in my class,
Hope it is my friend.
We've got a cross-country race,
I just know I'll be last!

Rachel McGoff (12)
Highdown School

SCHOOL

Schools have footballs
They are big or small
They are bouncy and soft
They are round and multicoloured
And you use them for football
And lots of other sports.

Ben Collings (12)
Holyport Manor School

MAN U

I like Man U 'cause they're the best,
So much better than all the rest.
The first team to win the treble
And they're always winning the double.

Beat the Gunners in the league,
The other teams don't get a peep.
They're scared of playing Man U,
Because they never know what to do.

Giggs is good on the ball,
Beckham is good at taking free kicks,
Forlan crosses the ball in the box,
Scholes with his feet, manages flicks.

They're the best in the world,
So much better than the rest.
Work well as a team,
That's why they're the best.

Peter Edwards (13)
Holyport Manor School

HALLOWE'EN

Creepy! Weepy! Sleepy!
A night to remember
A night of fright, creepy
Weepy, many kids on sight
Ugly witches - ghosts too.
Vampires so scary they always come to life,
Boo!

Tilly Gleeson (13)
Holyport Manor School

MY BROTHER

My brother is crafty
He is a complete pest.
He is always annoying me.
When he messes my stuff up,
I mess his back.
He fights with me,
I hit him.
He's a pain in the neck.
He's only nice when he gets told off.
But, we like each other really.
He can be very funny
And he spoils me sometimes.
He looks after me
And makes sure I'm alright.

Ravneet Bassan (12)
Holyport Manor School

FRENCH FRIES

My favourite food is French fries
They come from potatoes
Squidgy, squashy.

My favourite food is French fries
You can get them from McDonald's
Yummy, scrummy
My favourite food is French fries
Hot in my mouth
And they fill my tummy.

Julie Grant (13)
Holyport Manor School

Last Week

I started a bad week
School work
Homework
Friends
I didn't get things right in school,
Homework; I wasn't doing,
Falling out with friends,
Having a load of arguments.
Towards the end,
Everything became good.
I got my head down,
I picked up my school work,
Did my homework,
I stopped calling my friends names.
Friday is nearly here,
Yes! No school.

Daniel James (15)
Holyport Manor School

Crocodiles' Smiles

Crocodiles, crocodiles
They give you big, fat smiles.
Crocodiles, crocodiles
They eat piles.
Crocodiles, crocodiles
Never give them files.
Crocodiles, crocodiles
I love crocodiles.

Nathan Nuttall-Morton (11)
Holyport Manor School

About Me

My name is Jonathon
I have brown hair
I wear glasses
I use a walking frame

I use sticks to walk too
I can walk a few steps
But it makes me tired
I am a happy person

My dad is a funny man
He tickles me
Makes me laugh.

Jonathon Lewis (14)
Holyport Manor School

Maths

Maths is good
The teacher is great
She gives me merits!

Adding and subtracting
And the times table
Playing maths games
And work on the computer.

I do so much work
That I'm tired at the end
Of the lesson.

Craig Dowling (12)
Holyport Manor School

Horses

I've got fourteen horses at my horse ranch
Next Saturday we are getting a new horse
I ride and groom them every Saturday.
I like everything about them
Some horses are really cute
I think I might be getting one soon.
You can get lots of colours
Brown, grey, bay, black,
Chestnut, white and more.
I love horses so, so much
I know how to lead people
And I know how to tack the horses
I know how to catch them from the field.

Emma Clarke (13)
Holyport Manor School

Speed

A Ferrari speeding along the road
The wheels are spinning very fast
As the shiny red car zooms past.

A rusty old banger chugging along the road
The exhaust pipe, with smoke coming out
Slowly, slowly it goes *pop,* and I shout.

Pedalling very quickly
The wind blowing in my face
I love riding my bike, I win every race.

Wayne Ford (11)
Holyport Manor School

Myself

My name is Kelly,
I have brown hair.
I have brown eyes,
I am tall.
My favourite thing is listening to music,
I like the Sugar Babes.
I went to hospital
They took me into theatre.
I had an operation,
My scar is on my head.
It is much better.
My mum and dad said,
'You look much better now.'
I am happy I had it done.
I can look in the mirror now.

Kelly Wheeler
Holyport Manor School

My Cats

My cats are lovely and fluffy
My cats always purr and miaow
My cats have ginger, black and white fur
My cats have fleas
My cats have collars with telephone numbers
My cats drink water and milk
My cats go into other people's dustbins
My cats go into the garage
My cats eat meat and biscuits.

Michael Clare (12)
Holyport Manor School

Me

My name is Graham
I am tall
I am dark
I like books
I know a lot of things
I know a lot of facts.
I don't like going outside
I do like reading
Library books.
I like going on the computer
I like playing games.
My friends Kelly and Katherine
Say I giggle a lot.

Graham Wild (14)
Holyport Manor School

I Love Cars

I love cars.
The engine and body kit
All customised
The spoiler as high as your head
Dump valve
Drops take your last breath
Before the race begins.
Adrenaline kicks in
You're off!
Before you know it
You have won.

Matthew McRoberts (14)
Holyport Manor School

My Brother, Thomas Young

My brother, Thomas Young, he likes me.
He likes watching videos.
He has blond hair.
He is shorter and younger
His birthday is 25th October.

One day he got into trouble,
Dad shouted at him.
William is younger,
He goes swimming every Sunday.
He goes to school with Mum and Dad.

He has got a lovely face and blue eyes.
William plays with Thomas in his bedroom.
Thomas likes me to read a book to him.
Soon he goes to start to run.
He does love going in my bedroom,
He likes to go on the computer and plays games.

Karen Young (15)
Holyport Manor School

Smart Car

Blue, so shiny that sky has fallen.
Strong like a yoghurt,
good for parking in small spaces.
You can't go on holiday because it's so small
you cannot fit a suitcase in the boot.
Shaped like a box.
It's comfortable inside and it's full of leather.
Wheels are so fat and round,
the shape of the wheels makes you dizzy.

Colin Barron (13)
Holyport Manor School

My Mum

My mum is small
She is blonde.
She has blue eyes
She likes sitting down
When she has done the housework.
She also works
She works at embroidery.
She works hard
She is tired when she
Comes home.
When I am naughty
She shouts.
She was happy when
I had my injection.
She is a brilliant mum.

Greg Rackstraw (14)
Holyport Manor School

Football

I like football, it is cool
In football you should try your best
If you want to be one of the best.

If I had a wish my dream would be
That I could play for England
And be number 7
And as rich as Beckham
He curls the ball like no other
Oh how I wish he was my brother.

Ben Cripps (13)
Holyport Manor School

My Pets

I've got two dogs.
One is white
And one is hairy.
One is called Bo
And one is called Basil.
They bark for their tea.
I've got lots of fish
In a fish tank
In the kitchen at home.

Thomas Williams (11)
Holyport Manor School

Football

The players are warming up,
They're running onto the field
They're practising.
They're getting ready to play football.
They start playing with other teams
I like playing football with my friends.

Luke Risk (11)
Holyport Manor School

Me

My name is Amandeep.
I have very dark eyes
Sometimes I am funny
Sometimes I get into *trouble*

Sometimes I say the wrong things
I say I am sorry
Sometimes I do it again
I am learning.

Amandeep Maan (14)
Holyport Manor School

Me And My Two Sisters

I've got two sisters
Nicola and Emma
They make me laugh
We watch videos
We play music
Sometimes we go shopping
Sometimes we argue and then we make up.
I don't like going to school
I would rather be at home.

Tina Lewis
Holyport Manor School

Krystal

I like Krystal
Because she is lovely.
She is the prettiest girl
In the world.
Sometimes she's sad
Sometimes she makes me
Smile.
She is happy.

Mark Wilcockson (16)
Holyport Manor School

GRAND THEFT AUTO 3

The best game on the PlayStation 2.
I play it after school
You crash cars
You blow them up
Some cars are fast
And some are slow
Some race along
And some don't go.
There's a car called a Stinger
It goes really fast
Sets cars on fire
And the police chase you.

Chris Brown (11)
Holyport Manor School

DOGS

Some are short
Some are small
Some are long
Some are tall
They are scary
They are nice
They are cuddly
They are cool
Soft and fluffy
Huggable and furry.

Ravi Rajput (11)
Holyport Manor School

My Friend Stuart

Stuart is a friend.
He's a lot younger than me.
But age,
Doesn't matter to me.
He says,
He wants to live with me.
He says he likes me,
Because I'm kind.
He looks up to me,
As an older person.
He's always pleased,
To see me.
He likes having an older friend
Like me.

Matthew Graham (15)
Holyport Manor School

When I Grow Up

I want to be a helper
I can help my family
To clean up the house
And help Mummy and Daddy.

I'll polish the window sills
And wash the floor
Hoover the carpet
And wash down the door.

I'll help my sisters
Change the bed sheets
And then I'll sit down
And have a cup of tea.

Abbie-Gayle McCabe (11)
Holyport Manor School

My Mum

My mum is very good to me
My mum buys me sweets
My mum is kind to me
My mum always looks after me
My mum gives me pocket money.
My mum and me had an argument
And we were nasty to each other.
By the end of the week
We had made up
And we were nice to each other.
My mum buys me lots of things
And takes me places.

Matthew Marshall (14)
Holyport Manor School

I Wish I Was A Bird

I wish I was a bird,
Beautiful in flight.
I want to be a bird,
Soar to any height.
I'd love to be a bird,
Sleeping in a nest at night,
Please can I be a bird,
I'd be such a pretty sight!

Melissa Freeman (11)
Kendrick School

The Wave

Swelling
Like a secret
Shy, waiting to break free,
Then shimmering in opaline
Glory
It roars.
Silent thunder
Carries it to the sky
With Herculean strength, crying
Through wings
Of white.
A lullaby soars
In polyphony. Sounds
Of cathedrals falling vanquish the
Valleys,
Calling
The naiads to
The sea as orchestral
Clashes fall and fade to slowly
Subside.
Rainbows,
Piercing the spray,
Scatter stardust, fairy tears,
In the placid, wild caress of
The wave.

Bianca Summons (16)
Newlands Girls' School

Seasons Come And Go

The snow falls on a cold winter's morning,
Settling on the grass where the fresh dew lays,
In the bleak, dull sky the birds are soaring,
For today begins like the other days,
Birds brighten the morning and sing a tune,
For today is another winter's day,
Deep in the woods the snowdrops start to bloom,
Yet snowdrops and dewdrops are not to stay,
Fresh buds begin to form as spring appears,
Clenching on bare branches that winter leaves,
The frost on the ground is no longer here,
Spring is the time of year that you must seize,
The snow is melting and the sun is bright,
The leaves and the flowers are all in sight.

Kathryn Kellett (13)
Newlands Girls' School

My Sonnet

A sonnet is a verse with fourteen lines,
But for our homework we had to do eight,
On every other line you make it rhyme,
For inspiration I now sit and wait.

On every line there are ten syllables,
And every line contains five heavy beats,
The rhythm is quite tricky where it falls,
But end results sound great if it succeeds.

I want to write about the world outside,
But I can't seem to find the perfect word,
I want to curl up in a ball and hide,
This homework is the worst I've ever heard.

This sonnet now will really have to do,
But what grade will I get? I wish I knew.

Sarah Lewis (13)
Newlands Girls' School

DARK SPOT

No heart is pure, buried deep down within,
A dark dingy room with a long lost key,
Ready to be unlocked to release sin,
Sparked off by hatred, money, jealousy.
Knife in a back, blood staining the wooden floor;
A former lover, a breaker of hearts,
Found sleeping with his girl's best friend next door,
Killed in sudden rage by a thoughtless dart.
An unplanned murder sprinkled with regret,
Police sirens blare inside her confused head,
Panic-stricken girl runs off in cold sweat;
A young twisted face was found hanging dead.
Anyone could explode at any time,
A black spot can cause a disastrous crime.

Clare Third (13)
Newlands Girls' School

New York

If you look at the city of New York
Onto the streets where maybe you once walked
You'll see something missing, unseen, not there
It may seem to you a little bit bare
The towers and victims sadly perished
In our thoughts they will always be cherished.

The hatred is great for those Afghan men
For all we know it could happen again
Three minute silence we held with respect
For this fateful day those men will regret
When you look at the city of New York
Look a little closer, stop, think and pray
For all the victims on that tragic day.

Tara Bennett (13)
Newlands Girls' School

Feline Fantasy

A soft wet nose creeps from its velvet lair,
Nail-biting teeth that could rip through my skin,
Skimming through the forest like a swift hare,
Eyes as sharp and powerful as a pin,
A voice as gentle as a kitten's purr,
Padded paws that hide a hidden secret,
Glistening stripes fading down her bright fur,
An untrainable, vicious, killer pet,
Hiding so quietly, ready to lunge,
A cunning creature with a human's brain,
Into the lush water it loves to plunge,
A roar as loud as a person in pain,
Sliding through the forest that it smothers,
Tiger, tiger show your vivid colours!

Emma Bailey (13)
Newlands Girls' School

I Hate Spiders

Tall ones, short ones,
big ones, small ones,
ones with long legs,
ones with beady eyes
I hate spiders.

I hate spiders
They pretend to be dead
you prod them and they still don't move
but when you get a Hoover they panic and run.
The small ones aren't so bad
but the big ones are the worst
they scuttle to the deepest, darkest corner
where the Hoover can't reach.

I hate spiders
I switch on the Hoover.
The spider clings to the carpet
like a child clings to its mother on the first day of school
then . . . it's gone
sucked into the black darkness of the Hoover
to see the light no more.

Alex Murray (13)
Presentation College

The Rainforest

The rainforest glows green.
The leaf has a drop of water, but the stillness does not let it drop.
It is a dream with a different atmosphere, warm and wet and very tropical.
You measure the size of the rainforest with your distinguished eyes.
The green scenery makes it look like a bunch of grass.

Raja Afzal (13)
Presentation College

Scarlet Memorabilia

Walk out the door, my son
Break into a run, my son
Never again, my son
Never again

I wanted a castle
A velvet nothing
Bring me an eiderdown
So I can stop believing

It's not your fault you're lonely
You never had a chance
Have another drink
To help you draw the canopy

He said he was a wanderer
A walker of the night
A sailor of the stars
I never did believe him

She hides inside her stethoscope
Collecting scarlet memorabilia
Of all the things she's broken
Of all the things she's had

I never was one for moments
I never was one for fools
But all time has been a moment
And through all time I've been a fool.

Joss Bromley (13)
Presentation College

The Mystery In The Snow

I am big and furry.
Who am I?
I live on a mountain top high,
Watching the clouds go by.
Who am I?
I live on snow,
That is as white as my fur.
Who am I?
I have big sharp teeth,
But I won't eat you.
Who am I?
I walk upright on two legs,
Not on little pegs.
Who am I?
I hide away,
Until the warm weathers of May.
Who am I?
I have very big feet,
But have not walked on a street.
Who am I?
Where I live there is no time
And no money, not even a dime.
Who am I?
Some people think I'm imaginary.
Some people think I'm mean.
But no one knows,
Because I have never been seen.
Who am I?

Daniel Shojaie (13)
Presentation College

I Once Captured A Wish

I once captured a wish.
Wispy and light,
floating on a breeze.
I put it in a cardboard box
and fed it everyday:
Sunlight, laughter,
Optimism and truth.
And soon, I was the proud owner
of a dream.
I put it in a bigger box
punched with a few holes.
Gave it everything it needed:
treats of love and caring
and took it out everyday
to show it what could be done in the world.
It grew and grew.
It was brave and strong.
It challenged the world and
won.
No longer in a box,
I found,
I was the proud owner of
myself.

Ashley David Bryan (15)
Presentation College

The Photograph Album

They let you have your photos in the ward
I love to see how much the children have grown
And now my girls have children of their own
I like to knit for them, the shops I can't afford.

The photos show we celebrate the years
We celebrate the joys and times and births
And the weddings where we spread mirth
The smiling faces of our little dears.

I see my face much younger at my wedding
And Bert, now dead so handsome at my side
And Mother, I remember how she cried
And everyone said I was a lovely bride.

My daughters now are married, far away
And don't have time to see me every day
So I relive the celebrations my own way
Looking through my album, I wait till death takes me away.

Hugo Sharpe-Johnson (14)
Presentation College

What Am I?

I live in forests,
Cold and wet,
Near rivers and streams,
What am I?
Some people fear me,
But others cuddle me,
What am I?
Some people call me a grizzly . . .
What am I?

Geoffrey Joseph (13)
Presentation College

Wind

Wind that no one can see,
Howls through the night,
Giving everyone a fright.

Wind that no one can see,
Plays with the kite,
Helps with the flight.

Wind that no one can see,
Breeze as in slight,
Hurricane as in might.

Wind that no one can see,
Cold as in bite,
Warm in the sunlight.

Wind that smoke gives away,
You are my delight,
My heart you ignite.

Lara Jones (12)
St Bernard's Convent School, Slough

The Sky

Blue is the sky
Which the birds use to fly
Some evil hunters take aim and fire
They kill them to their desire

Blue is the sky
Which planes use to fly
Some evil passengers scheme and plot
And deter fliers a lot

Blue is the sky
The whirling blades go by
As the helicopter swoops through the air
Often when off to war they fly in pairs

Blue is the sky
Which many years ago dragons used to fly
Now they are no more
And we take to the sky ever more.

Kevin McCormack (11)
St Bernard's Convent School, Slough

HERE THEY GO!

Bounce! Smack! Goes the ball
Smash! Bang! Goes the wall
Peep! Peep! Goes the train
All day in the rain

Punch! Kick! Goes the man
Glug! Crack! Goes the can
Broom! Broom! Goes the car
Going to a place so far

Bite! Scratch! Goes the cat
Fly! Fly! Goes the bat
Ring! Ring! Goes the phone
With its new and improved ring tone

Click! Click! Goes the pen
Buck! Buck! Goes the hen
Fly! Soar! Goes the plane
All the way to Spain

Michael Blanco (11)
St Bernard's Convent School, Slough

The Pair Of Shoes

Once there was a pair of shoes,
that liked to walk round on their own,
they walked all around the town,
but always found their way back home.

It was quite a funny sight,
to see these shoes walking round,
trudging through all the shops,
making not a single sound.

They went into all the shops,
but first was always Clarke's,
they were looking for a family,
but trying not to make footprint marks.

When they got home,
they always took a giant leap,
back into the porch,
where they fell into a dreamy sleep!

Danielle Betts (11)
St Bernard's Convent School, Slough

Summer

Summer is like a young boy,
Who plays with his best friend, the sun.
Together they play all day
And have lots of fun.

Summer never feels cold,
He never feels less than warm.
He's always felt this way,
Since the day he was born.

The only time Summer is sad,
Is when Winter arrives.
He bullies Summer and sun
And ruins their lives.

But, although they are upset by
This, as it makes them very sad.
Winter only comes once a year,
So it's not all bad.

Graham Ashton (11)
St Bernard's Convent School, Slough

THE SWEETIE TRAIN

As the sweetie train comes down the track
full of sweets, green, yellow and black.

There's gummy cars and jelly beans in jars.

There are sugar bears and fruit flavour pears.

The strawberry laces and jammy faces.

And of course the lollipops with the chocolate drops.

The candy sticks and the multicolour pick 'n' mix.

Not forgetting the lovely gingerbread men and the rainbow drops
in packs of ten.

And did you know that the chocolate mice are really nice, the
smarties for the parties and sweets for treats.

And . . . then . . . when the engine powers up its steam,
Please say I am not in a dream!

Andrew Young (11)
St Bernard's Convent School, Slough

A Barren, Desolate Land

Silently, stealthily, I soar
Through the barren, desolate land
Filled with shiny monsters.
One of them stirs.
I wait with anxious anticipation, cautious curiosity.
It spreads one wing, then roars like a spitting volcano.

Its eyes illuminate with anger
It has not fur not feathers nor skin
But armour resembling that of an armadillo
That glints in the midday sun.
I remain fixated on this exquisite creature
Suddenly, it emits a menacing growl, then charges.
It speeds up, its scornful eyes jeering at me
I do not have time to fly away. It has caught me.

I hit it with a splat,
It hesitates for a brief moment
Then activates its windscreen wipers.

Nicholas Ivison (11)
St Bernard's Convent School, Slough

A Magical Night

When I look up into the sky
I see
A magical new place to me
Such a wonderful sight
The stars shining bright
Like diamonds lighting up the night.

When I look up into the sky
I wonder
About the planets far away
Is there life out there? I ponder
For it all looks such a dazzling sight
When I look up into the sky at night.

Tanya Kalyan (12)
St Bernard's Convent School, Slough

The Moon

The silvery orb,
The shimmering light,
Falls upon the cold, dark night.

The soft, white beams,
The mysterious glow
Drift along, to and fro

A flighty moth,
Happy and confused,
Dances in the light
That brings good news

The news is of
The light it loves,
Luring it to fly above

The moon, the king
The shining light,
Dazzles, sparkles, shining bright.

Amika Chaudry (12)
St Bernard's Convent School, Slough

COLOURS

Red is the sunset as pretty as can be,
Yellow are the feelings that live inside me.
Pink is a pig living in a sty,
Blue is the colour of the never-ending sky.
Green is the grass growing on the lawn,
Brown is the colour of a baby fawn.
Gold is a ring on a lady's hand,
Black is a horse standing tall and grand.
Silver is the moon far away in space,
White is the colour of embroidered lace.
Grey is a rain cloud floating on air,
Cream is a little sheep's matted old hair.
Purple is a plum hanging from a gnarled tree,
Orange is the sun, tanning me!

Harley Panioty (12)
St Bernard's Convent School, Slough

A BOWLING ALLEY

Can you hear . . .

The mechanical doors sliding across the floor when activated?
The gasps and the 'oohs' when the shoes are chosen?
The music that the shoes and the floor create together?
The chatter of the balls waiting to be chosen?
The thuds when the balls hit the floor of the lanes?
The bangs when the balls crash against the sides of the lanes?
The laughter of glee from the skittles when they are knocked over?
The sighs of happiness when the balls fall onto the conveyor?
The creak of the machines when they replace the balls,
The sweaty 'phews' when the bowling shoes are returned?

Becky Matheson (11)
St Bernard's Convent School, Slough

ME

I hope this is a dream,
I really cannot cope.
I hope it doesn't seem
That I'm a royal dope!

My grandma's giving me lessons
On how to act right.
I wish she'd stop these sessions,
They're giving me a fright!

My dad is depending on me,
To make something of my life.
I wish that he would stop
Putting me through all this strife!

I wish that Lily
Would come back and be my friend.
She's being so silly
And is driving me around the bend!

I hope I can be normal,
After all, I'm only a kid.
I don't want to dress too formal,
I just want to be . . . me.

Anya Gogna (12)
St Bernard's Convent School, Slough

TIME

Time goes, time comes,
even when you're having fun.
The games you play
the things you say,
but you want to stay
and say hip, hip, hooray.
You go out, you come in
just don't chuck time in the bin.
The thing you want to skip is . . .

Homework!

That's the thing you can't skip
even when wobbling your hips.
So keep time safe,
play with your mates,
don't let time go past
'cause it goes very fast!

Moral: Don't waste time.

Helen O'Horo (11)
St Bernard's Convent School, Slough

WAR

Thousands of soldiers march through the night,
With pride and courage their hearts are alight.
Striding on towards the fight,
To help England in its plight

At the centre of terrible violence,
Gunshots and screams heard in the distance.
Heroes' hearts are very tense,
As the trembling battlefield turns to silence

The soldiers return very mournfully,
Back to their home, back to their family.
The war has been ended but very painfully,
Hundreds sacrificed just for a victory.

War is wrong.

Michael Dixon (12)
St Bernard's Convent School, Slough

THE BUILDING

I pass it everyday,
Early though, so it isn't very exciting,
It's lit up,
Its strange lights surround its obscure shape.
'I like it,'
I say out loud.
'What is it like during busy hours?'
I question myself.
I feel adventurous.
'Maybe . . .'
I decide to slip out of school at lunch to see what it's like.
'What?'
I feel someone doesn't agree.
I need to know, I feel it's my duty.
I plan my escape,
I plan my story.
What if?
Oh no, I feel scared.
It's an adventure,
I reassure myself,
And I go through with it.

Harriet Costelloe (12)
St Bernard's Convent School, Slough

TRAPPED

I was trapped
Sitting on my kitchen chair,
It pounded against the ground.
I looked out of the window gloomily
Waiting for it to stop.

To pass the time, my homework was done,
But still the pitter-patter droned on.
Bored out of my wits, nothing to do
And still it wouldn't stop.

The day was getting on,
It would soon be dark,
My hope was gone
For the rain would not stop.

But in the end I got my reward
My friend came over,
We had so much fun
Even though the rain would not stop.

Brendan Durkin (11)
St Bernard's Convent School, Slough

AUTUMN

Autumn is a colourful time of year.
The leaves on the trees are golden
And when they fall to the ground,
They are crisp and form a rustic-coloured carpet,
When walked upon they make a scrunching noise.

Autumn is a beautiful time of year.
In the morning the grass glistens with dew,
The sun shines gently
And the air is fresh,
A soft breeze fills the streets.

Autumn is a wonderful time of year.
The sky is covered in white fluffy clouds,
With tints of blue peering through.
Most people are wrapped up warm,
Trying to avoid the coming of Jack Frost!

Rebecca Ryan (11)
St Bernard's Convent School, Slough

When I Close My Eyes . . .

Once everyone has gone to bed
and the lights are out
I close my eyes
and listen out.

When I close my eyes
I can hear the clock
that ticks every second
and never seems to stop.

When I close my eyes
I can hear the cars
that go whizzing down the street
very, very fast.

When I close my eyes
I can hear the rustling of the trees
that is being made
by the wind and breeze.

When I close my eyes
I'm there by myself
then the sounds start to fade away
and I'm left there to sleep.

Lauren O'Keeffe (11)
St Bernard's Convent School, Slough

Nobody Cares

Nobody cares if you're down and out
Nobody cares what you're about
Left alone on the street to die
Who really cares, you or I?

How did he come to live on the street?
Circumstances he came to meet
How sad things never went his way
Let's hope things get better, I pray.

The tragic thing about a down and out
Is that they never seem to have their shout
Helpless, unhappy and feeling alone
Do you ever hear them moan and groan?

I'd like to help them if I could
But where do I start and do you think I should?
That's just what everybody says
Julie, Mary, Mark and Les

So nobody helps the down and out
Nobody cares what they're about
But I'll do my best to help them a little
To strengthen the faith that is so brittle.

Katrina MacKay (11)
St Bernard's Convent School, Slough

HAMSTER OF MINE

You're small, orange and white,
With silky fur and a little button nose, that wiggles all the time.
Sometimes I get such a fright
When you jump off the sofa and disappear.

You have a funny walk, which I call a waddle,
You go round and round on your wheel and rush through plastic tunnels.
You get me in such a muddle
When your sharp teeth chew the bars of the cage - are you trying to escape?

You love your treats, but so many end up in your pouch
A tiny tongue licks at the water bottle,
Everyone would vouch
You're cute.

Always sleepy, never awake except at night
I look for you, but you're hidden in sawdust and bedding
I know that you're alright
Such bright eyes, but I know that you can't see far.

You lean into the food bowl
And top it all off with a hamster treat
You dig so well you're like a mole
And finish the day off with a quick groom.

Elaine Robinson (11)
St Bernard's Convent School, Slough

WHY CAN'T THEY JUST UNDERSTAND?

How can people live like this?
Guilty of a crime,
How can they get out of bed?
Without understanding, not knowing
What's in their victim's head?

How can they live normally?
Not thinking what's wrong with me,
How can they live with what they've done?
How can they walk beneath the sun?
How can they actually sleep at night?
Knowing they can't do anything right,
Why can't they be more like you and me?
All they need is to be able to see,
What's going on in our heads,
When terrorism grows and we are left dead.

Shani Connors (11)
St Bernard's Convent School, Slough

MY TRUE FRIEND

Forever and ever I will think of you,
Cos you friend have and will be true.
You always cheer me up when I'm down,
I think that you could turn the world around.

Not one time have you been sour,
You make me smile around the hour.
You and I will stick together,
Through heavy rain and bad weather.

Why I deserve you, I've no clue,
A piece of my heart you will take with you.
Everyone should have a friend like you,
But you are special and there's nothing I can do.

Millie Fitzmaurice (12)
St Bernard's Convent School, Slough

The Cheesy Sock

At the bottom of my dance bag,
There is an old and smelly sock,
You think it is just a plain one,
But it will give you quite a shock.

For if you look through a glass,
Then you'll surely see,
It houses a lot of people,
As tiny as can be.

Their eyes are red and stare at you,
Can't you make the link,
They make their hands bold and blue,
Until your face goes pink.

They live in houses made of mould,
With beds of fluff and dust,
Eating bits of crisp and cake
And sarnies without crusts.

Now it is time to destroy,
The aliens from space,
I hope they don't come back to me
And see my bright pink face.

Serena Mills (11)
St Bernard's Convent School, Slough

I AM

I am a million things at once or
Nothing at all.
I am, I am, but am I?
The diamonds that make the sea
Glitter.
The oasis of the desert traveller.
Something carried on the wind
Is it,
Laughter or
Weeping?
The colours of the ever-changing
Rainbow
The sighing of the
Mountains.
The wings of the
Swallow
So free, so very free
I have seen a thousand things
What was, what is, what will
Be.
I move, indeed I am always on the move
But am I fast or am I slow?
I cannot tell,

You shall not know.

Emma Schofield (12)
St Bernard's Convent School, Slough

Remember Me

Remember me,
In the spirit of the wind,
In the laughter of a child,
In the waves of the sea.

Remember me,
When happiness is gone,
When the nights are dark,
When you are alone.

Remember me,
When the rain is falling,
When the sun is shining,
When clouds are grey.

Remember me,
In a flock of birds,
In wild horses galloping free,
In the dolphins swimming gracefully.

Remember me,
When you look at the stars,
When you see fresh water flowing,
When you see the flowers in the field.

Remember me,
When I am gone.
Remember me.
Remember.

Jo Mitchell (12)
St Bernard's Convent School, Slough

TREES

As I walk,
Through the rustling trees.
I can feel
The cool autumn breeze.

The leaves are
Copper-red and golden brown.
It's such a shame
They have to fall down.

Winter is here
As cold as ice
Nothing looks as
Colourful and nice.

The trees now
Have nothing to wear
Their branches look
Naked and bare.

Fortunately spring
Will soon be here
And everything beautiful
Will reappear.

The trees' leaves
Will soon be seen
A fantastic variety
Of shades of green.

Laura Szeder (11)
St Bernard's Convent School, Slough

Me

Here is a poem all about me
All about me . . .
As you will see . . .

I like to swim in the sea
While laughing and talking with lots of glee
This is the poem all about me . . .

I like to watch TV
And it always makes me sleepy
When I watch documentaries . . .

I love to watch The Simpsons
Marge, Maggie, Lisa, Homer and Bart
And I think it's funny how Bart's not all that smart . . .

I like to eat
Sometimes before I sleep
But I hate to eat red meat . . .

I am a lazy boy
And I love playing with toys
But never with ones that make noise . . .

I am not keen on sports
And sometimes I forget my shorts
Then I will end up in a different sort . . .

Now you've heard all about me
What I'd like you to see
What it's like to be a Veazey . . .

Christopher Veazey-Doucet (12)
St Bernard's Convent School, Slough

LIFE AS A ONE-YEAR-OLD

As a baby what I see,
Is a stalker who follows me.
They were there in every place,
That I happened to face.

I move my arm and so does he,
All he does is copy me.
It's not my dad or my mum,
I'm so scared I could suck my thumb.

If my mum or dad had said,
It was a mirror by my bed.
And in the bathroom and downstair,
It wouldn't have taken me unaware.

I love the park, there's so much to do,
Picking flowers, chasing quack, quacks too.
Things to climb up and fall off as well,
Argh! There's someone coming on a bike with a bell.

When Humpty Dumpty fell off the wall,
Was he pushed or did he fall?
And Little Miss Muffet is always scared,
After so long she should be prepared.

My first Christmas is in December,
A special day to remember.
All I could think of was the cunning plan,
To mess up the decorations if I can!

Emma Cunningham (12)
St Bernard's Convent School, Slough

LIFE AND DEATH

What is life if it leads to death?
We're just passing through, what will life bring?
There is no night without dawning,
No winter without a summer or spring.

When they come into this world,
You're happy; you hear their first word, their purr,
But if you love someone let them run free,
If they come back, they're yours, if not they never were.

'We're not here for a long time,
We're here for a good time,' said that man to me,
Lying on his deathbed, full of pain,
But still he smiled with glee.

'Why are you so happy?' I asked him,
A tear ran down his face,
'I'm loved immortally by my family,
But I'll go to a better place.'

A wink of an eye and he's gone out cold,
He's left; he's far away from me,
Far with God on the cloudy tops,
But how far from me can God be?

If God is with you all the time,
Then the old man to me is still near
And finally in my mind a shadow appears,
I'm filled with sadness and fear.

If God takes you over a snowy mountain,
You see the footprints of your life,
Yet there's only one set through the times of rough,
He carried me through my troubles and strife.

Kiera Underwood (11)
St Bernard's Convent School, Slough

POEM ABOUT PLANTS

Plants come in all shapes and sizes
Tall or short, fat or not.
Some grow in the ground,
Some are placed in a pot.

Some plants have flowers
Some plants have leaves,
Small plants like daisies
And tall plants like trees.

Some plants stick to certain heights,
Sunflowers can be small,
Where as some can change
And be very, very tall.

The colours can vary
To be dull or to be bright,
Petals and leaves are coloured
To be dark or to be light.

There is a tree with yellow, green and red,
There is a plant with white and with pink.
You can make pictures with flowers
On fields, use them as ink.

Some float on water
Like water lilies,
Floating on ponds,
Attracting the bees.

Some flowers are used to symbolise things
Like weddings for happiness.
Or funerals for sorrow,
Or even a gift for kindness.

Chloe Hutchins (12)
St Bernard's Convent School, Slough

Unicorn

Thump! Thump! Thump! Thump!
Coming nearer, coming soon.
Thump! Thump! Thump! Thump!
Wild as the rising moon.
Stumbling, crying, bleeding, dying.
Ever headed to her doom.

Thump! Thump! Thump! Thump!
Horn amongst the swirling mist.
Thump! Thump! Thump! Thump!
Ever ceasing to exist.
Disbelieving, e'er deceiving,
Always, still, ever a myth.

No longer seen, no longer heard,
The unicorn is riding on.
But all those minds that don't believe
Just help her along.

For she is on the path to death,
For she can no longer be seen.
She'd be taken in, be tested,
Hushed up, hidden behind a screen.

The unicorn is of the forest,
The unicorn is wild and free
And though it is the saddest truth,
She knows it is her destiny.

Thump! Thump! Thump! Thump!
Shimmering shadow, white as snow.
Thump! Thump! Thump! Thump!
Seeping life her soul will go.
Ever fated, breath is bated,
We forget her full of woe.

Laura Mountford (11)
St Bernard's Convent School, Slough

I Love You

We've been through a lot,
You and I,
But we've kept going,
Past the low and high.

Not knowing when this long,
Winding road will ever end
And through those lonely nights
You've been a good friend.

Over those many moments
That have turned to years,
You've helped me survive and
Overcome my fears.

When the world seemed dark,
You were my only sun,
But I've never really told you,
I love you Mum.

Rebecca Le Flufy (12)
St Gabriel's School, Newbury

Spring

Spring dodges,
Through flower beds,
Making their petals bloom,
He waters and feeds them generously,
Washing away all gloom.

Spring skips,
Through fields and meadows,
Brightening up the sky,
Bringing joy to everyone,
And no one ever cries.

Rachel Morgan (12)
St Gabriel's School, Newbury

Topsy-Turvy Land

The people walk on their heads
The people look through their feet
The trees are made out of sand
In Topsy-Turvy Street

The children go to school by night
And the owls come out by day
Kids drink tea, adults drink juice
In Topsy-Turvy Way

The bus stop's out at sea
The water's what they're going through
The boats go over miles of land
In Topsy-Turvy Avenue

Less flavour than an apricot
Vindaloo is bland
Water is quite spicy hot
In Topsy-Turvy Land.

Natalie Hyde (12)
St Gabriel's School, Newbury

Excitement

High above my head,
soaring through the air,
no wings, no support,
just me holding on.

My heart is beating fast,
I feel like an eagle,
I can't control myself,
as I rise towards the clouds.

I look up further to the sky,
now the clouds are closer,
I'm still flying, gliding, riding,
all around the sky.

Now the day is over,
I come back down to earth,
I touch the ground carefully,
and pack up for another day.

Beth Robertson (13)
St Gabriel's School, Newbury

The Cat

She wears only the finest furs and the most expensive necklace.
She keeps herself clean and tidy and is always well turned out.
Her hair so sleek and shiny
Her eyes sparkle bright.
Curled up by the fire wearing her best white slippers,
While her rhythmic breathing fills the warm air.

Katie Lyons (13)
St Gabriel's School, Newbury

Spring

Spring jumped
Through the scented meadows
Touching budding flowers
Filling each one with happiness
Bobbing and singing in the breeze.

Spring danced
Around the lamb-filled fields
Like a ballerina
Skipping and turning in the wind
With kindliness in her heart.

Spring raged
Around the woods like thunder
Thrashing the Earth with rain
Creating the paths through the forest
Fighting against all evil.

Rebecca Brown (13)
St Gabriel's School, Newbury

My Cat Tom

Heat-loving, grilling,
Milk bowl spilling,
Purring, softly spitting.
Claws, like needles knitting,
Sofa cushions scratching,
Teeth like daggers catching.
Tom, my favourite cat.

Charlotte Gent (14)
St Gabriel's School, Newbury

The Shooting Star

It is a dark navy night
When every star is out.
The moon looks like a silver horseshoe
That is gleaming from every angle.
I can see gold dots,
The size of a peppercorn
Waiting to be crushed.
Suddenly I see a shooting star,
It is different from all the rest,
But it is coming further
Down, down, down, down!
I can see it on the pavement now,
No one else has noticed.
I rush out of my house to get it,
But it's not there!
It must have been in my imagination.
I go up and up into my room
And it's there!
But oh no!

It's a dream.

Catherine Ramsbottom (12)
St Gabriel's School, Newbury

Fear

An icy river oozes through my veins,
With a chilling wind, it creeps up my spine,
Its strong, stony fingers claw my face,
Thundering footsteps crowd my heart
As a silent tear trickles down my cheek.

Beth Tilley (13)
St Gabriel's School, Newbury

Big Ears

They think I'm large and stupid,
but I'm actually big and wise.
They say that they protect me,
but I know that that's all lies.

I love to munch on green leaves
and paddle in the stream.
I like to blow my trumpet loud
and make the humans scream.

I'm a very happy creature
and I'd never hurt a fly.
I try to live in happiness,
but they just make me cry.

I run fast when I want to
and I can be a great friend;
helping creatures out of trees,
the desert I defend.

Just cos I have big ears,
doesn't mean I'm Noddy's friend.
I despise those humans
because I know they'll be my end.

I'd just like to be left alone,
without them watching me.
They say this is a free world,
but where's my privacy?

So next time you see an elephant,
remember these wise words:
we can get very angry
and we travel round in herds.

Steph Poulson (13)
St Gabriel's School, Newbury

HER FIRST PAIR OF SHOES

These are the shoes
She ran around in
When we played
Around the house
When her playroom
Was full of mess
When she learnt
To tie her laces
When her knee
Got grazed
As she fell
Running to me
When she pushed her first pedal
When she was late
For nursery.
These are the shoes
She toddled about in
And I've kept them
In my room.
These are not the shoes
She wore when I went
When she asked me where
I was going
That she heard
My footsteps leave
When she asked me
To send her a postcard.
These are not the shoes
That she wore when she left
But she'll want them
When she comes to me.

Karan Rai (12)
St Gabriel's School, Newbury

AUTUMN

Autumn brings
Winter onto the stage
Clears off all the leaves
Autumn is Winter's showgirl
Presenting him to the world.

Autumn kicks
Up the red and brown leaves
Raked into a pile
Swirls them in a whirlwind
Blowing quite a gale.

Autumn hides
The wild forest creatures
From the shooting gun
Deer and fox seek shelter
In Autumn's shortened days.

Naomi Rowe-Gurney (12)
St Gabriel's School, Newbury

FEAR

Fear lives inside me and multiplies when I'm alone,
Fear is when a car slows down when it passes me,
Fear is when the phone rings, then stops dead,
Fear is when I hear footsteps behind me walking down the street,
Fear is when the lights go out and I'm on my own,
Fear is when the door opens and there's no one there,
Fear is when a shiver ripples down my spine,
Fear is when my heart beats faster than before,
Fear is just a figment of my imagination;
It's not there after all.

Gemma Phillips (13)
St Gabriel's School, Newbury

TAKING PLACE

First dew on the first grass
The first bleat of the first lamb
The bursting blossom on the first tree
The sparkling sunlight on the first green leaves

Sunny, sandy beaches, the smell of BBQs
Fields of golden corn sunflowers facing the sun
Yachts drifting on the wide open sea
Those were the happy holidays

As I walk along the road there is a crunch of
Leaves beneath my feet
The colour range is amazing; red, yellow, orange, brown
Then suddenly a gust of wind picks them all up
With just the conkers left rolling along.

Trees like sticks, widespread arms
Ready to grab you at any second
Frosty icing coats the forest
Glad we collected the logs when we did!

Charlotte Horner (11)
St Gabriel's School, Newbury

MUM'S MOOD

Threatening black clouds,
A rainy day ahead,
Nasty weather approaching,
I feel like going back to bed.

It traps me inside,
I can't phone up my mates,
My brother's on the phone,
My room is in a state.

The loud and nasty rumbling,
Is coming up the stairs,
I'm not really that scared,
But I hate the way she glares.

It's outside my door,
It's quieter now,
The bad weather's gone away,
I can go out to play.

Lucy Hammant (13)
St Gabriel's School, Newbury

TOO LONG

It's been too long in here,
So many days gone by,
One, two, three (I can't remember).

Our candle is going down
down
down

Mother is getting tired looking after me,
Sometimes I wish she was in a safe place,
Enjoying herself, not worrying about me
And especially Father.

I was going to go to another home,
But Mother was too afraid to let me go,
Like Father was let go.

It's been too long in here,
So many days gone by,
One, two, three . . .

Alison Noble (14)
St Gabriel's School, Newbury

THE SUN

Opens in the morning light,
Smiles gleefully, the sun so bright.
It sways across the silent air,
The shining light, way over there.

The misty fog blocks its view,
It seeks a passage, peeping through.
Taking a yawn, ready to go,
The shining light swoops so low.

Looking out and seeing down,
A little beam brings on a frown.
I miss the lovely blaze of yellow,
Which was so sweet, so gentle and mellow.

Trishil Main (13)
St Gabriel's School, Newbury

NO ONE SPECIAL

I'm only one person,
One drop in the ocean,
One of many more fish in the sea.
One ear of the corn,
One raindrop in the storm,
So why do they care about me?

I'm not the most pretty,
I'm not the most clever,
I'm not the best player at sport.
I'm not the most cool,
Of the girls in the school,
So why do they give me a thought?

Jessica Welch (12)
St Gabriel's School, Newbury

World War II

Ding-dong,
Shuffle, shuffle,
Clip-clop,
Here comes the boy again.
'Please sir, anything on offer today?
My mum is dying and my dad is fighting,
We need some food I pray.'
'My dear boy, my stock isn't here,
The merchant ships have sunk.
No supplies this week, I fear.'
Bang, smash,
Dear oh dear,
They hover around in the sky,
Why don't they leave us alone?
Lots of innocent people will die
And listen to all of those cries!

Jasmine Orton (13)
St Gabriel's School, Newbury

Evacuees

I stood on the platform,
With my luggage in my hand,
Feeling like an unwanted toy.
On my right was a little boy,
Clinging to his mum,
To my left was a little girl,
Eating a sandwich.
The atmosphere was tense and cold
With the thought of leaving,
What will I do without my mum and dad?

Tasha Westall (13)
St Gabriel's School, Newbury

If I Wake

Tell me, why do we fight
Why do we sleep through restless nights?
And in the morning if we wake
Why are we taught to hate?

For through the deep blue nights and darkened skies
The moon will glow and the sun will rise
But in my bed I will lie,
As if to hide my pain inside.

So what is love when war is here?
A moment of happiness, in a world of fear.
As youthful minds bring dangerous thoughts,
For over time they've not been taught

That they can't possess one another,
Nor will they be in this world forever
But the damage they cause and the hate they make
Will stay in this life and circulate.

So when this godforsaken world has died,
The last baby born, the last tear cried,
I will place my soul to rest
On the last gravestone left.

Georgina Le Flufy (14)
St Gabriel's School, Newbury

Alone

Her crinkled and aged fingers,
Twisted the wool with her needles,
Her face was crumpled like a brown paper bag,
She was alone in the room.

Creaks from her rocking chair echoed through the house,
Rocking backwards and forwards,
A sharp shock then struck her like a dagger in her heart,
She was dead in the room.

Sarah Duggan (12)
St Gabriel's School, Newbury

TOXICITY

The wind whirled down the streets,
He whispered to the buildings,
The cold, bare bricks,
The empty windows.
He gave up and moved on.

The wind flew down the road,
He murmured to the trees,
Lifeless, deep in
The toxic earth.
He gave up and moved on.

The wind swirled round the people,
He tugged at their colourless clothing.
They stared at their feet,
They hurried along.
He gave up and moved on.

The wind crept down the alley,
He echoed through the night,
He circled the dust,
Dead leaves and rubbish.
He gave up and moved on.

Caroline Wilson (12)
St Gabriel's School, Newbury

The Battle Of The Roses

White rose, your elegance and beauty,
Your silky, pearl-white dress,
Your wonderful true cleanness,
Fills the room with your happiness.

Red rose, your deep-red blood,
The darkened side of hope,
You the gift for your loved one,
Before you do elope.

Pink rose, you do surprise me,
What is your meaning now?
Hope? Love? Happiness? Sorrow?
To you I certainly bow.

The battle of the roses,
Is always going on,
Which will you give your loved one?
Forever is so long.

Alice Stirmey (12)
St Gabriel's School, Newbury

Spring

Spring prowls,
Through parks and gardens,
Lapping up the cold,
Racing and running everywhere,
Turning the frost into sun's gold.

Spring whips
And glides through forests,
Scampering up the trees,
Singing, playing and dancing,
As it's no longer the season to freeze.

Spring dines,
In the light of the sun,
He hurries away
When it's colder again,
As it's the end of Spring's fun.

Holly Woodhead (12)
St Gabriel's School, Newbury

KEY OF DREAMS

As night surrounds me,
I search in my mind,
I search for the key,
To release my dreams.

Open the door, key, open the door!

As slumber comes I find the key,
Moulded in silver and gold,
And in the heart of this key,
Is a pair of fluttering wings.

Open the door, key, open the door!

I take the key into my hands,
And unlock the secret door,
A door that reveals many lands,
From the recesses of my mind.

Open the door, key, open the door!

I enter the land of dreams,
Of adventure and daring deeds,
Where nothing is what it seems,
A new world to see,
A world just for me.

Clarisse Loughrey (12)
St Gabriel's School, Newbury

THE BUTTERFLY

If he were a person,
He would be an acrobatic pilot,
Entrancing people while he is in flight,
Doing dangerous somersaults in the air!

If he were in a house,
He would be in a painting,
Letting people look at him,
For longer, maybe even forever!

If he were the weather,
He would be an early autumn day,
With his body like a fallen leaf,
Flying, twirling, moving through the air!

If he were a colour . . .
Well, I really couldn't say!
Because he could be many, even a lot,
All of them patterned on the butterfly's wings!

Kate Mitchell (12)
St Gabriel's School, Newbury

AUTUMN ANIMAL

Sharp and alert,
Quick and swift,
Hangs from trees,
Moves like a drift.

A gatherer of nuts,
Grey as mist,
Red as a fox,
Tissy, Tiss, Tiss.

Hides among the leaves,
Climbs along the branches,
Hides in little holes,
Among the twigs he dances.

You'll miss him if you blink,
Quick and swift,
The squirrel in the autumn,
Moves like a drift.

Catherine Hill (12)
St Gabriel's School, Newbury

TIGER

He stalks the night and lights it up
With his fluorescent orange back
And long, silky stripes

His paws tread softly across the
moonlit ground
As he approaches, animals scatter
Fearing his attention

His bright, staring eyes hunt for his
next victim
Ears prick up at the slightest sound
As he prepares to pounce

A great disappointment lurks in the
shadows
And disappears into the morning
As he drowns in his hungry sorrows

The sun begins to rise
Just another night gone by
For a fearless tiger.

Rosaleen Morshead (11)
St Gabriel's School, Newbury

THE PARADE

My excitement,
The thrill of seeing her.
Impatience in the crowd around me,
Suddenly
The famous music begins to play,
She's coming,
Her ears appear above the throngs of people,
The red bow starts to emerge,
I long to see her face.
Pushing, shoving, trying to get to the front of the crowd,
Fear of being squashed by the giant grown-ups,
All of a sudden I see her,
I can't believe my eyes,
It's Minnie!

Charlotte Keast (11)
St Gabriel's School, Newbury

SUBMARINER'S FAMILY

The silent water laps at the land,
Sparkling sea glistens below,
Emotions well up inside,
A black silhouette breaks the horizon,
I wave frantically in hope,
Certain he can see me,
In seconds it's beside the shore,
I yell in excitement,
All too soon the moment's past
And for seven long months,
He disappears beneath the waves.

Becky Thomas (11)
St Gabriel's School, Newbury

EARLY THAT CHRISTMAS MORNING

My eyes were drawn open by the sunlight
Streaming in through the opening in the curtains.
I stumbled into my parents' bedroom,
Found them sleeping deeply.
Woke them quickly with a shake
And quickly hopped down the stairs.
There I saw it, there it was,
A parcel all for me.
My parents hurried me on to open it
And quickly so I did.
So big, what could it be?
Inside I found a play kitchen for me,
I spent all the afternoon making cups of tea.

Emilie Atkinson (11)
St Gabriel's School, Newbury

DROWNING

I am drowning,
Lost in a sea of my thoughts.
I am sinking,
Under the waves of my dreams.
I am falling,
Through undulating darkness.
I am crying,
But no one can hear.
Drowning,
Sinking,
Falling,
Crying,
Gone.

Bronwen Edwards (12)
St Gabriel's School, Newbury

The Leopard

Lying on a thick branch,
Its tail swinging gently like a pendulum.

Dark brown rosettes glow warmly
On its deep yellow coat,
As the sun shines through the leaves.

I stare softly at its big, golden eyes
And as it stares back,
A warm feeling rushes through me.

Its ears twitch as its nose
Picks up a scent.
Alert, it jumps down,
Landing silently on the grass below.

It turns towards me
Before majestically walking
Deep into the darkness of the bushes.

Helen Warwick (13)
St Gabriel's School, Newbury

Living Book

Stars shine among the words,
Ivy crawls about the pages,
Out upon the cover
March armies of past ages.

Bats huddle in the index,
Lions prowl at the glossary,
While lurking on page twelve,
A forest of moss and tree.

At third chapter, ocean,
At appendices, there is sea.
And when it declares 'The End',
There stretches eternity.

Ailsa McCaughrean (12)
St Gabriel's School, Newbury

SCHIZOPHRENIA

My world is my reality,
It's where I love, it's what I see.
What can be more real than that?
It's you, him, her and me.

They insult the intelligence of my mind,
When they look and stare so rudely,
They see me as mad, but I'm just creative,
And yet they treat me so cruelly.

What people classed 'normal' cannot comprehend,
They simply push aside,
They label us 'random', when really the truth is,
We come more regularly than the change of the tide.

Like the flickering colours in a candle,
We just bring more colour to the world,
We are not insane nor crazy,
We are not twisted nor curled.

Why can't people see us as we are,
Humane as the rest,
Who are they to judge us anyhow?
Everyone's different if put to the test.

Chantelle Davison (12)
St Gabriel's School, Newbury

CATS

Curled up tightly around each other,
They lie on the end of the warm, cosy bed.

They lift their heads to look at me,
As I quietly switch on my music.

I climb gently onto my soft, comfy bed,
And lay my head near theirs.

I hear their soft, tranquil purring,
As I lean up close to them.

I stroke their soft, furry heads
And tickle beneath their chins.

They rest their heads back down on the blanket,
Close their curious eyes
And drift into a peaceful doze.

Lucy Peacock (11)
St Gabriel's School, Newbury

THE FOX

This is the fox that was happy,
When he jumped and played around all day,
When he curled up safe and warm at night,
His bushy tail wrapped round his once alert face,
The moonlight shining on his orange back,
When there was nothing to worry or trouble him,
When he learnt to hunt with his brothers and sisters,
When his home was quiet and peaceful.

This was the fox that was born happy,
Before his life was wrecked and destroyed,
Before he was hunted and killed for living,
Before he was chased and tracked for fun,
Before his life became a constant struggle to survive,
Before every second of his day was a misery,
Not knowing when he would be hunted next,
Until he wished he would die.

Natasha Turner (12)
St Gabriel's School, Newbury

ROMANCE

The bud of the rose is like love at the start,
Petals opening bring joy to my heart.
The soft, smooth petals, they bloom before my eyes,
People we care for, we idolise.
The vibrant colours make my heart sing,
I hope one day I will possess a ring.
The perfume of this lovely flower,
Alas, my head is dizzy with its power.
As time goes by the colours fade,
Just like my thoughts begin to shade.
As autumn arrives each petal dies,
Can this affair withstand the cries?
Suddenly the flower has gone,
This prettiness doesn't last so long.
The thorns are left,
The beauty hidden,
My love is over, all thoughts forbidden.

Sophie Matthews (13)
St Gabriel's School, Newbury

The Netball

The ball whizzing, speeding,
Cutting through the morning air
Like a swallow, darting,
Heading home.
Players passing, hand to hand
Willing it down the court.

The goalpost's hungry mouth,
Waiting to be fed.
The hoop of hope.
The final thrust.
The rustling of the net,
On the cold, September morn.

Helen Brandwood (12)
St Gabriel's School, Newbury

Loneliness

Closing in on me,
Darkness between four walls,
A prison cold and bare,
Trapped behind bars.

Creeping in on me,
Shadows stalking me,
A wall, blocking me
From the outside world.

Sneaking up on me,
Gloom visits me,
Left discarded,
Day after day.

Sophie Kilduff (14)
St Gabriel's School, Newbury

THE SEA PIPERS

Voracious waves crash to the shore
Clawing at their victims ravenously,
The undulating sea flounders
On the rocks, showing no mercy

But still the ghostly pipers keep on piping,
Luring, with eyes of deceit, foreboding and
Mysterious.

Ostentatious, the temptress sea entices the
Oblivious into death's flamboyant fiction,
The theatrical ocean applauding and rehearsing
For the next scene

But still the ghostly pipers keep on piping,
Luring, with eyes of deceit, foreboding and
Mysterious.

Fishermen are beckoned,
But never return
Falling into the depths of eternity
Their souls are restless, crying out in despair

But still the ghostly pipers keep on piping,
Luring, with eyes of deceit, foreboding and
Mysterious.

Alice French (12)
St Gabriel's School, Newbury

THE TREASURED ITEM

These are the wellies
She rarely took off
The wellies she wore
To clear out the loft
These are the wellies
She wore for walks
The wellies she held
When we had talks

These little red wellies
Were red and shiny
With Postman Pat
When she was tiny
These wellies would receive jokes
And now and again
Soft little pokes

These were the wellies
She loved like a toy
These tiny wellies
Were her pride and joy
But when she went
She left them with me
So in my mind
Her I could see.

Oriana Williams (11)
St Gabriel's School, Newbury

THE ICE-SKATES

These are the ice-skates,
That are shimmering bright,
Blades cut the ice,
Like a crystal on glass,
Skater spinning,
Jumping through the air,
Atmosphere palpable,
Emotions running high.
The crowd cheers,
The lights blink,
She spins,
A pivotal moment . . .
Dream or nightmare?

She leaps to her fate,
Time suspended
Until her ankle crumples,
The look of pain
Shattering all hopes.
She plunges earthwards,
A broken twig in a hungry gale,
She will discover that this
Is to be her last fall.
These are the ice-skates,
That shared her defeat,
Rusting, unnoticed,
No one cares where.

Claire Nicoll (11)
St Gabriel's School, Newbury

EXISTENCE

I am in the middle
In the middle of the street
Everyone's walking
Walking past me.

Hurrying, running
What's their rush?
I am waiting
I'm not rushing.

I'm paralysed, stunned
Scared, still
Staring, watching
I've no movements.

Though I'm worth nothing
They look at me
They give me strange looks
Such bemused looks.

I've nowhere to go
I'm so confused
What do I do?
I don't understand.

I'm here in the middle
The middle of nowhere
Everyone's looking
Looking at me.

Emma Constantine (12)
St Gabriel's School, Newbury

DREAMING

Dreaming . . .
Of the gas mask
I pulled over my face at school.
'Does it fit?'
They asked.
The leather scraped my face.

Dreaming . . .
As I walked home I saw
Children being evacuated and
Soldiers getting on
And off the train.
I walked a little further
And passed a shop. I saw a
Bar of chocolate through the window.
My mouth watered and my
Tummy rumbled
But I had no money.
I walked a little further
And started to climb onto
Some sandbags and rubble.
A soldier came and said,
'Unexploded bomb! Go away!'

I walked through the front door
And my mum was buttering
Some scones for my tea as a treat.
It seems like an ordinary day
Not like we are at *war.*

Charlotte Povey (13)
St Gabriel's School, Newbury

Red Snow

Bare feet stepping on the snow,
As a thin crust of ice crunched beneath her,
Barely a sound disturbed the air,
As hair whipped around her.

Eyes danced as wild as fire,
Her hair was as black as night,
Her skin and gown were icy white,
As she watched her prey draw nearer.

An icy rock sliced the air,
A hiding place,
A place of death,
It was here the hunter waited.

He pranced delighted in the snow,
His laugh as bright as glass,
Joyfully he stepped,
Toward the concealed danger.

The air was crisp,
The snow was white,
The sky shone red with anger,
A piercing scream split the air as danger leapt towards him.

Away she stepped her gown dyed red,
Her bare feet silent on the bloodstained snow,
Barely a sound disturbed the air,
As hair whipped around her.

The sky and snow shone red with blood,
The rock like a sacrificial altar,
His heart and throat lay torn on the ground,
So laugh he could no longer.

Nicky Markides (12)
St Gabriel's School, Newbury

SAILING

The waves pounced and snarled against the side of my boat
like wild tigers.
I rose and tumbled, soaring as high as a bird, then falling like a pebble.
The rain beat down on my soaking back and lightning crashed
in the dark sky.
My boat was a tiny ant in a desert, abandoned and not knowing
where to go.

The waves stroked and purred against the side of my boat
like an embracing cat.
I sailed across the calm, smooth waters as if I was sliding over velvet.
The pale sunset, its colours leaking into the sea, fell slowly
to the depths of the ocean.
My boat was a fugitive from its old life, waiting to explore
a new culture.

Kirsten Riddick (11)
St Gabriel's School, Newbury

FIRE

I am red-hot,
I burn on the spot,
You may think I am cold
But boy, can I scald.
I twist and I turn,
I churn and I burn,
I engulf you with flames,
But don't take the blame,
For you know it was me! It was me! It was me . . .

Catherine Okell (12)
St Mary's School, Ascot

FEARLESS?

His arm outstretched, sword in hand.
Fearless, he creeps cautiously through the rain-drenched trees.
The echoing hoot of a far off owl comes rushing through the
Forest of Dread.
He is fearless, but for how long?
Now whispers engulf the sodden trees.
Whispers, whispers of what?
His heart begins to race, but still he carries on
through ancient dwellings of the long dead.
He senses motion in the trees behind him and spins round . . .
nothing!
He breathes a heavy sigh of relief and continues his perilous journey.
Then the battering armies of the wind
bring him the smell of fresh blood.
His heart pounds faster as he breaks into a wild run,
a run to meet his doom.
Then his pursuer looses an arrow.
It lands right on target, piercing the young man's armour
like a knife through paper.
With a strangled scream, the fearless knight, son of King Arthur,
collapses in a dead heap to the floor.
Evil has won this time and the forest is silent once more.

Emily Girkins (11)
St Mary's School, Ascot

HATRED

Anger, loneliness, fear, depression,
Screeching, whining, screaming, pining
Hate
Black and grey, brown and red,
Foggy, misty, storming, dead
Hate

Early in the morning, late at night,
Kicking, biting, nipping, fighting
Hate
Bloodshed, killing, swords and daggers,
But worst of all words
Hate.

Henrietta Scrope (11)
St Mary's School, Ascot

ALONE

Waiting till they get back,
Heart thumping hard like a lion pouncing on its prey
Trapped inside this prison until they get back.
The door creaks open,
Curtains blow wide,
My throat gulps again

Floorboards creak as if someone is behind me.
Daring not to look.
Phone ringing like a piccolo playing in my ear
Answer it! No one the other end.
My throat gulps again

Unexpectedly,
Lights go out,
The phone cuts off,
Television blacks out,
Clock chimes twelve.
A picture flashes from the window;
Only lightning; I wish.
A knock on the door.
My throat gulps again.

Annabelle Thomson (12)
St Mary's School, Ascot

Carrots

Sitting on a cold damp shelf,
Waiting to be grabbed,
Someone please come and take me,
Stop being so picky,
Waiting day after day,
Finally I get plunged into a trolley with a bundle of stuff.
What is that red light that just struck me?
Pushed into a plastic bag, placed into the back of a car,
Zoom, off I go into the giant house,
Being taken out of the noisy bag,
Placed over a smelly ditch,
A metal sharp thing comes shooting towards me
Peel, peel. Argh! What are they doing?
A great shiver ascends my spine.
Whoo! They have finished.
Thrown into a giant jacuzzi,
Bubbles floating everywhere,
Placed into a cold, china dish in the middle of the table.
Crunch! I disappear.

Lauren Davis (11)
St Mary's School, Ascot

The Graveyard

Grey, crumbling graveyard,
With a house perched on a hill,
Hears whispers, sees shadows, but tells nothing.
Cobwebs guard the shadowy corners. Still.

Outside the wind circles the swaying trees,
A phone is placed on the floor
Dusty, silent, unplugged.
The licks of darkness seem to tease.

It suddenly jumps to life
Ring, ring, ring,
She answers just as I expect
She says, 'Hello, who's there?'
I breathe back, 'This is your worst nightmare.'

Georgina Kelly (11)
St Mary's School, Ascot

FIRE: FIEND OR FRIEND?

Fire is bad
Death
Poisonous
Dragon-like flame.
Danger
Destruction
Venomous snake.
Burning heat
Explosions and bombs
A lizard of rays and flames.
Cans and cans
Of fuel and gas
This causes fire
It's not a hard task.
But . . .
Fire is good
A warning
A light
Food and a weapon.
This is fire.

Eloghene Otobo (11)
St Mary's School, Ascot

Cookies

Thud! In goes the boulder of butter,
crushing the pebbles of flour.
Then, an egg is beheaded on the side of
the bowl, followed by it's yolk dribbling
down the side.
A hail of sugar is quickly added,
splintering the mixture and bowl.
Plop! A large wooden spoon is stuck in
the swamp and struggles to relieve
itself. The paste reluctantly gives in
and the spoon dances freely.
A snow of chocolate chips stands clear
in its way and it begins to struggle
again.
But all is calm, liquid is here to save it
from a horrible death.
The spoon begins to spin around faster
and faster; splashing in a flood of milk.
It digs into the mixture and places a
wood on a new field.
Once entered, a volcano begins to erupt
around it.
The crowded place heats up and the
substance goes hard, and there:
a pile of cookies.

Helena Stefanowicz (11)
St Mary's School, Ascot

THE GECKO THAT DIDN'T DIE

'Look! Look!'
'I've seen it before.'
But I looked again before it was no more.
This gecko with his sticky feet,
Before he had time to scurry and fleet.
He had just climbed up a crooked wall,
When a bird took advantage,
Because he was small.

That night while I prayed,
For his awful life,
All I could think of was his trouble
And of my strife.
I made up a tale,
It was short and quick.
The bird picked him up
And after a while he fell, slick.

He ran back through the forest wide
And encountered dangers
From which he had to hide.
When he reached the edge of these big trees,
He ran home and avoided some bees.
There his wife tucked him into bed,
'My dear where have you been?' she said.
'My dear of my troubles I'll tell you tomorrow.'
After that I slept well and had no sorrow.

Davinia Goodhart (12)
St Mary's School, Ascot

My Perfect Lunch

Plop! In goes the baked beans
Heavy like a waterfall
Bright orange, they splash everywhere in the saucepan
It is tough to stir at first; it takes an effort.
Down goes the bread into the toaster
Ting!
The kitchen starts steaming
I can smell the juicy baked beans.
My mouth starts watering.
I can hear the bubbles from the beans.
Steam rises into my nose
Ting!
Up pops the toast.
On a plate goes the toast, the baked beans fall on top.
Down into my tummy it all goes
And there I have my baked beans on toast.

Camilla Wright (11)
St Mary's School, Ascot

Who's There?

Creak! Goes the step as I clamber down feeling my way through this blanket of darkness.
Tick, tick, tick goes the clock in the distance of the room.
Whoosh! Goes the curtain as a chilling breeze comes flying through the window.
Bang! Goes the door as it is forced open by a powerful gush of wind.
Squeak, goes the rusty hinges of the door as someone shuts it.
Boom! Boom! Goes my heart as I take a step forward, terrified.
Rustle, rustle. Something moves in the never-ending blackness.
Who's there?

Ella Hadsley-Chaplin (11)
St Mary's School, Ascot

The Bowl

The flour gets sieved into me, *patter, patter.*
The sugar comes next and flops on top.
Egg looms towards me, bumps into me and the rain
of white and plop of yolk makes me sticky.

The spoon rotates my floury, eggy side.
Milk pours in, whitening everything like a
snowstorm,
disturbing the still peace of before.

The spoon's still going round and round and round,
making me dizzy.

I'm tilted and all my insides cascade out.
Washed and dried, I'm put on a shelf.

Louisa O'Connell (12)
St Mary's School, Ascot

Storms

A storm is brewing.
Big, black clouds come.
Cats run for shelter
Doors open and close
Excited lightning flashes through the sky.
Falling rain hits the ground.
Gales blowing leaves away.
Havoc spreads far and wide.
Indigo, blue and green colours.
Joyful cries throughout the land.
Keen children begging to go outside.
Lovely colours in the sky
Musical sounds fill the sky.

Mara Ticzon (12)
St Mary's School, Ascot

The Invasion

It starts just a glimpse,
A flicker in the darkness.
Its growth disturbs the peace.
Expanding
Parading
Enveloping the blackness.
Ascending into the dimly lit sky.

It dances,
Jumping, leaping, fluent, flowing.
Fluttering, in the raging light.
Flexible, beautiful,
Yet evil, destroying.
Violent, invading
The piteous houses with a tidal wave of
Gold, orange and heat.
It burns, it breaks and . . .

Gone
Disappeared - water its enemy.
It leaves as quickly as it comes
And the lamentable ruins
Once fresh built houses
Have turned to ashes.
New healthy oaks
Have turned to dust;
And what it leaves brings sorrow.
'Fire,' they cry
Begging for sympathy,
But the damage is done.

Eleanor Drage (12)
St Mary's School, Ascot

THE SCREAM

Awake!
A scream from the woods,
Slipping on my dressing gown,
I open my bedroom door,
Another scream.
What is happening? Who is screaming?

I creep down the stairs. Wait!
It could be dangerous.
It is too late now.
I walk through the kitchen and out the front door,
Through the garden and into the woods.

Cold, wet, horrified,
I walk quickly on the damp leaves.
Suddenly, I see a quick, swift movement,
Something is close, there is an opening.
My heart is pumping, harder and harder.
One more step to reveal who or what is there:
I step.
Something rustles.
My legs want to stay but my mind is curious . . .
Is this the end?

Noises of rustling, squeaking and death fill my ears,
Out comes a small, orange object.
It is a fox!
Lying, licking its paws.
It had screamed a fox scream, looking for a mate.

Michelle Katz (12)
St Mary's School, Ascot

Pizza

Twirling round goes the dough
Slap onto a cold, damp surface.
Dollop, gooey tomato sauce is
Firmly placed onto a thin bed.
Spread and smooth the sauce is flattened,
Sprinkle, sprinkle thin strips of yellow rain,
Bed into the fine sauce.
Chop, pepperoni slices,
Drop onto the thin strips of yellow rain,
Lifted onto a warm tray.
Into a hot sauna it goes.
Slam, it is trapped.
Hot, hot, boiling, boiling.
Creak, the door is opened,
It is put onto a board.
Slice. Melted, steamy cheese oozes
Over the side of the knife.
Grab; the pizza is gone.

Chelsea Power (11)
St Mary's School, Ascot

Dawn

An angry, blood-red ball rises,
It illuminates the stony hills and turns the rivers to gold.
In the valley of darkness down below, where the light lies strewn
In patches. A gaunt face is stretched across the sky.
With nerves of steel and eyes of steel dawn has been aroused.

Iona Seligman (12)
St Mary's School, Ascot

SUNRISE

The sky was bright and the Earth was warm
In poured light on this summer morn
The scarlet sun stretched out in the sky
Where not so long before the moon had been gazing by
Glistening dew covered the emerald grass
And I watched as a flock of birds flew past
The sky now auburn showed the leaving of dawn
And the hummingbird's song showed that this day was born
The moment was indescribable in the beauty it portrayed
This bright sunrise was the best time of my day.

Olivia McLoughlin (12)
St Mary's School, Ascot

UNICORNS

With their fur all sleek and white,
Their manes all shiny and silver,
The great horn reflecting the light,
As they wade through the river.

The whinny, though soft and quiet,
Can be heard by others all around,
Dragons, birds and other creatures,
Hear it glide along the ground.

As it gallops unseen by humans,
Across the grassy ground,
It's golden hooves making no sound,
Even though we can't see it,
We know it's there:
We can feel it.

Emma Dudley-Hammatt (11)
The Abbey School

TALKING

My best friend likes to talk.
She can chat and chat forever and ever
about anything and everything.
Me? I say nothing!

She doesn't notice my silence at lunch.
She's chattering nineteen to the dozen.
She's used enough words for me and her
and I say nothing!

I can't get a word in edgeways.
She won't let me reply.
She wouldn't notice if I died right now.
But I say nothing!

My best friend hasn't stopped talking yet.
I don't think she can stop.
Her chattering's driving me nuts,
so what can I do but yell, 'Shut up!'

You would think she'd shut up wouldn't you?
For just a little bit.
Does she take any notice?
I think I'm going crazy!

Pim Fitzpayne (11)
The Abbey School

LIFE

What is life?
Fair or unfair
Happy or sad
To make mistakes or to learn mistakes

To be good or bad
To enjoy it or not
To love it or not
But that is life for *you?*

Cleo Lyn (12)
The Abbey School

WEEKENDS

At the weekends,
I go to the pool,
I swim lengths and widths
And look such a fool.

At the weekends,
I watch TV,
EastEnders, Simpsons,
And CBBC.

At the weekends,
I go to the cinema
To watch Lilo and Stitch
And to eat lots of popcorn.

At the weekends,
I go to my mates,
Or my friends come to mine,
We eat sweets and watch Blind Date.

At the weekends,
I go to bed,
And brush my teeth,
And cuddle my ted.

Alexandra Rankin (12)
The Abbey School

THE LAKE

A mist lay over the motionless lake,
A ghostly, shrouded figure,
Its hands wisps of condensed cloud,
Its breath felt like ice against my cheek.

I fingered a smooth, red pebble
Saw its speckled surface
Disappear into the murky, inky black lake
As I let it slip slowly from my hand.

I sat hugging my knees to me,
As the wind picked up,
As it savagely beat at my small figure,
Contemplating, pondering.

I glanced higher into the foreboding sky,
The clouds stirred angrily,
Witches brewing up a tempest,
Restless and brutal.

The mountains towered above the lake,
Imposing and awe-inspiring,
Their edges, durable, serrated,
Breaking holes in the rampant clouds above.

I rose, my hair flying wildly about me,
The wind grabbing at me frantically,
The atmosphere pressing upon my soul
And I smiled.

Rupinder Kaur (12)
The Abbey School

HOMEWORK

Going to school is bad enough,
but homework is a bore.
English, maths, science,
French and many more!

We normally have one hour,
but two hours at weekends.
I wish I could have fun instead,
it drives me round the bend.

We have maths homework twice a week,
the lessons are bad enough!
Algebra, tables, fractions and
other complicated stuff.

I can't get out of learning French,
bonjour and s'il vous plait
we write it in our vocabulary books,
to learn for a test next day.

Then there's English, not too bad,
poems, drama and prose.
We study plays by Shakespeare,
Not too bad, I suppose.

One day I will finish school,
my homework terrors will end.
Then I can tease my little brother,
I bet it will drive him round the bend.

Clementine Wilding-Taylor (12)
The Abbey School

First Impressions

T he first day is drawing near
H appy? Sad? Filled with fear?
E veryone smiles to be at school.

A ll the day is really cool.
B ut the first day's speech, how
B oring and long,
E specially with the headmistress droning on.
Y es, at last it's at an end.

S o back to the form room it is,
C hatting really loud,
H appily, I find a friend called Georgia.
O h, so many children,
O h, I am so proud.
L aughing, we exit the school.

Happy and cool!

Cléa Heaton (11)
The Abbey School

Charlotte

(Dedicated to Charlotte Wiggins who moved to the Middle East in August 2002 and is greatly missed)

C razy and wacky,
H elpful and kind,
A mazing at swimming,
R emembered by everyone,
L oads of laughter,
I mpossible to forget,
E ventually, she'll come back!

Alice Wein (12)
The Abbey School

I Am Here, Where Are You?

Is anybody there?
Does anybody understand,
That my life is drowning me deeper
And I need a helping hand?

Does nobody out there listen?
Does nobody hear me cry,
As I struggle for safety,
Before it's too late and I die?

Can nobody out there see?
Does anybody watch my pain,
That seeps through my eyes
And trickles down the drain?

Is there anybody out there with feelings?
Does nobody care that I'm lonely,
Left lying in the gutter,
Under children glaring stonily?

Can anybody out there smell?
Can't they scent that grotesque fear,
That sends me to sleep crying,
Never knowing what is near?

Does nobody out there taste?
Can't they taste the bitterness,
The cruelty I receive,
The sins they commit, yet don't confess?

Will I still be here tomorrow?
Will they let me live that long
And instead of turning away in disgust,
Come and sing me a song?

Emily Wright (12)
The Abbey School

Celebration Of The Seasons

Which season is my favourite? I just can't decide.
Look below and you will find,
Why I just can't make up my mind.

Spring season, fresh and new,
Lots of baby animals to play with you.
While the flower buds are forming,
By the fireside we're still warming.

Summer season, warm and bold,
Distant memories are the frost and cold.
Flowers which are very pretty,
Brighten up the towns and city.

Autumn season, crackle and crunch,
Squirrels storing up food for a winter's lunch.
Cold, damp mornings waiting for the bus,
Fireworks and bonfires as treats for us.

Winter season, white with snow
Jack Frost makes the icy winds blow.
Advent bringing Christmas cheer,
Then we celebrate New Year!

Belinda Tonkins (11)
The Abbey School

Princess

I want to tell you something about a girl I met in my youth
I swear on my mother's grave, that what I speak is the truth.
Her hair is a stream of golden clouds, wafting around her head.
Her throne engraved with pearls and laced with purple thread.
Her robes a rare silk and her gown a fine satin blue.
The chain around her neck is symbolising all she speaks is true.

Her shoes are a purple, a colour of strength and true love.
Her gloves are so elegant and in tiny stitches, is one baby dove.
She was my help and my comfort along the harsh, windy road.
She was there to help me when I fell and to lighten my load.
So if you see this maiden sitting with her hair like fine gold.
Then you'll remember this poem, that I once, was as well told.

Jennifer Duke (11)
The Abbey School

PEACE

The world would be a better place if *peace* ruled the world,
Many people wish for *peace* more than anything else.
Peace isn't an easy concept, you've got to work hard for it,
But when *peace* is in your heart, you'll be happier before you know it!

Peace is so important in our world,
We need it so much.
Without *peace* our world would be a disaster,
And lives hell.
Without *peace* in this world, it gives sufferings and hearts condemned,
That's why we pray for *peace* in our lives everyday.

In our world there's no such thing as *peace,*
Countries and families pray for *peace* everyday.
Peace is not revealed, but war is prevailed.
There's war in villages, towns and countries,
Where *peace* has never lived and never shall live there again.

Without *peace* in our homes and lives, there's arguments and distress.
Without *peace* in our world there's fighting and war.
Peace is here to stop that and to keep us all together,
Without *peace* what would our world be?

Lavanya Vimalan (12)
The Abbey School

HAVE YOU EVER WONDERED?

Have you ever wondered what it's like for me?
To only come to someone's waist,
When people see, they look at me,
Then suddenly walk on in haste.

To never be able to run like you,
Or play games and go and have fun,
To never be able to shout and leap,
When the school day is done.

I happen to be just a normal person,
Except I've only got one,
One little leg that's all it takes,
To start people making fun.

Have you ever wondered what it's like for me,
To only have one way to go around
And that's in a wheelchair so everyone stares,
So next time you see me give me a wave,
It's just to the wheelchair I'm bound.

Victoria Smith (12)
The Abbey School

SONNET FOR MEMORY

I will not betray you; I swear as long as I have breath
I will keep our pact and shed not a tear,
for that I should grieve over you was once your greatest fear;
it will be as you wanted, from this day until my death.
How can you be gone then, if I still live? I know you did not leave
or I should not still be here to hear their lies,
but not an angel in Heaven shall ever hear my cries
though my soul should shatter with your memory.

You are in the red rain of autumn that falls softly about me,
you are in the dusk, that timeless, tender calm;
you are there evermore to guide and cheer me,
my guardian, my energy, my friend, my balm.
And when I run or laugh or dance in the rain
then you are there beside me, and you live again.

Tessa Baker (14)
The Abbey School

Phases Of One Girl's Life

She is young.
Inside of her,
Her heart lies.
Inside of her,
It jumps, it pries - for more knowledge
And everyone can see it in her eyes.

She is a bit older now -
Inside of her,
Her heart lies.
Inside of her,
It gasps, it sighs - it weeps, it cries.
But why can't people see it in her eyes?

She is even older now -
Inside of her,
Her heart lies,
Inside of her,
It slows, it tries - so hard to stay alive.
But it can't hold on, it peacefully dies.

Marina Leoni (12)
The Abbey School

DESTINY

Destiny is the future,
who knows what it will hold,
sweets or parties or shopping trips
or your lunch will turn to mould!

Adults often say, 'You can't go out to play,
it's going to rain, you'll get really wet!
That's what the TV says for today.'

But what if you could make
the weatherman say,
'I can't predict the weather cos,
I could be wrong and what a price I'd pay!'

The future holds worries too,
'what if' and 'but it could . . .'
forgetting a camera on a wedding day
or a picnic basket with no food.

A storm could brew at sea
or a car engine could fail
when you're on your way to a football match
or even an auction sale!

But if everyone worries about the future
and if all your time is spent
on packing a camera or sandwiches
who's going to worry about the present?

Sara Valente (12)
The Abbey School

MEMORIES OF AN OLD WOMAN

Many, many years ago,
When I used to run,
Up and down the streets of London
So my chores were never done.

My mother used to scold me
And call me, 'Naughty girl.'
But then one day my daddy died,
She and I broke down and cried.

We had received a letter from Berlin,
It had my daddy's chinstrap in.
It said my daddy was good and brave
And for this country he died to save.

He never had a funeral,
For his body was never found.
But to this day, I have his strap
In a little pot, silver and round.

No longer up the London streets
Do I carelessly run.
My bones are now too old and weak
For anything so fun.

But at least now I know
That Heaven is not so far away.
And neither is my daddy . . .

Hannah Sawford (13)
The Abbey School

Seasons Are Turning

Spring has arrived,
All fresh and green.
Buds bursting open,
Eager to be seen.
White, fluffy lambs
Leap around the fields.
Happy and joyful,
Spring's here at last.

Golden, bright sun,
Hot summer days.
Lovely bright colours
In flowers and trees.
School days are gone,
Holidays wait.
Ice cream and beaches,
Summer has come.

Golden ripe corn
Ready to reap.
Red, juicy apples
To be gathered in.
The leaves turn brown,
Yellow and red.
Reaping and ploughing,
Autumn harvest.

Cold, frosty days
The trees stand bare.
White blankets of snow
Covering the paths.
Icicles hang,
Mince pies are hot.
Children go skating.
Winter draws in.

Christine Taylor (12)
The Abbey School

Bob

I once knew a man called Bob,
He was a great big snob,
He lived in a terrible old bog,
He once went out in the fog,
And tripped over a log,
He got bitten by a dog,
And escaped by having a jog.

Henry Morley (11)
The Oratory School

The Four Seasons

Against winter's gust
A happy face appears
Playing and enjoying

In the scarecrow's field
An invigorated bird rustles
Through the evening breeze

In the summer's eve
A bunch of crows appear
In the farmer's fire field

With all trees leaves
An autumn's breeze fills the air
With anything that is light.

Oliver Carrier (12)
The Oratory School

Rhyme And Rhythm

One waving wand
Two rippling ponds

Three flying bugs
Four sailing tugs

Five fighting kings
Six flapping wings

Seven silver swords
Eight dusty boards

Nine shining cars
Ten drinking bars.

Guy Woodeson (11)
The Oratory School

GOLDFISH

My
Headbutting
Goldfish
Bubble, splash
Zoom, smash!
Wet floor
Goldfish
No more

My
Headbutting
Goldfish
Bubble, splash
Zoom, smash!
Broken bowl
Death toll.

William Doe (11)
The Oratory School

MY PETS

Mokey
Always inside
Trying to hide
From going outside
Drives people crazy
From being so lazy
Eats lots of food
Always in a mood
She is my cat
Mokey

Harry
Small and cute
Never on mute
Always out in the rain
Must be insane
Has fluffy ears
Chases deer
He is
Harry.

Bertie Baker-Smith (11)
The Oratory School

BLACK AND WHITE

Black is fear,
Fear brings darkness,
A sign of death,
The shadow of happiness,
The bad memories.

White is gladness,
Fun in the snow,
A cloudless sky,
The stretch of a beach,
A shooting star,
A colour it can't always be.

Black and white brought friction to life,
TV and photos, a colourless fight,
A zebra in the bush,
The colour of sadness and glee.

Adam Marcus (13)
The Oratory School

PRIMARY COLOURS

The trumpet of a daffodil heralding spring.
The dying embers of a roaring fire.
The glare of the sun reflecting off snow.
The rivers of sunflowers lining French hills.
The strong scent of a yellow lily.
A meadow straddled with buttercups.
A shaft of sunlight penetrating the clouds.

The blue of the Mediterranean Sea with the rays gliding in and out.
The tint of ice, a frozen lake.
The sparkling colour of a newborn baby's eyes.
A clear sky on a frosty morning.
The ink flowing out of this pen.

A tractor crawling over a field.
The deep glow of an evening sunset.
A single poppy standing strong in a field.
A small sail just topping the horizon.
A fire engine whizzing past, sirens blazing.

Gareth Barlow (12)
The Oratory School

PRIMARY COLOURS

A fire burning at night,
The flowing blood of a soldier,
A poppy in a field of war,
The smell of a spring rose,
A sign of danger and anger.

The sky on a summer's day,
The bed of the great sea,
A violet in the dark wood,
Dolphins piercing the water's surface,
Rain that beats as it hits the ground.

The sun's rays bouncing off the Earth,
The stars shining out brightly,
The spotlight on the lead role,
A dancing buttercup,
A sunflower turning up to the sky.

Michael Hennessy (12)
The Oratory School

PRIMARY COLOURS

Blue:
A bright sky obscured by mist,
A deadened sea filled with fish,
The hidden gem covered with blue,
A happy chest at the depths of the lake,
A dark blue fish swims in a pack.

Yellow:
A gleaming daffodil in the light,
A yellow fog hovers over a morning rock,
A dazzling sun gleams on your face,
A shining chick with its mother,
A joyous chest crammed with gold.

Red:
A fire blazing in the depths of Hell,
A red poppy on a battlefield,
A brilliant sunset over the hills,
An autumn leaf falls to the floor,
A giant red house in the middle of the street.

Sean Desborough (12)
The Oratory School

PRIMARY COLOURS

Red:

Satan surrounded by the flames of Hell,
A postbox standing proud and tall,
Rows of poppies upon a battlefield,
The lively red sunset against a dull evening sky.

Yellow:

The sun beating down on the desert sand,
A monkey peeling a banana hastily,
Spanish sunflowers swaying in a cool breeze,
A block of gold for an Egyptian prince
And a cutlass of a ruthless pirate.

Blue:

The light blue seas of a tropical coastline
And the transparent summer's day sky,
The ink inside my very pen,
The baby blue eyes of a charming princess
And the tip of an icy mountain.

James Richardson (12)
The Oratory School

PRIMARY COLOURS

Red:
The beautiful sunset colours in the sky
A raging fire that burns into ashes
The red-eyed tinge of a giant coloured snake
The penetrating stare of a poisonous creature.

Blue:
The never ending depth of the deep blue sea
The dark blue in the starry night
The chilly colour of a polar ice cap
The spout of water from a giant blue whale.

Yellow:
The golden sun that sinks below the horizon
The yellow T-shirts of happy children playing
The glint of diamonds deep down in the mines
The yellow light shade of bobbing daffodils.

Oliver Kersey (12)
The Oratory School

PRIMARY COLOURS

Red:
Fire burning at the foot of Hell,
Angered faces darkened the mouth,
Rotten apples fall to the ground,
Blood smears on an injured boy's knee,
A poppy survives in a field of death.

Blue:
Icicles hang over endangered seas,
Frozen feet walk lands of snow,
Windy skies make swaying trees,
Waves crash on sandy shores,
75% of our globe's surface.

Yellow:
A blazing sun that lights up the Earth,
A bright eye catching colour,
A golden chariot racing in a circus of Rome,
A tiny match flame burning its way down,
A little sunflower glowing in the grass.

Henry Lake (12)
The Oratory School

The Seasons

The cold frost outside
The snow lying on the ground
Looks like winter's quilt.

A newborn baby
Hatching from a cosy egg
Its first sounds bring joy.

The sun rises high
And heats the wonderful world
People celebrate.

The leaves become orange
Days are getting much colder
School's about to start.

Adam Jennings (12)
The Oratory School

Rhyme And Rhythm

One speeding car
Two bendy bars

Three tubby pigs
Four Christmas figs

Five silly kings
Six seagulls' wings

Seven small cuts
Eight crunchy nuts

Nine seeing eyes
Ten yummy pies.

Edward Rowell (12)
The Oratory School

BLACK AND WHITE

Black is the colour of an Italian's hair,
Mourning and grief,
A newborn puppy,
And leather boots,
Ink that comes out of a pen,
Unexplored space and the universe.

White is the colour of hope and peace,
Wedding dresses and snowdrops,
Dalmatian puppies when they are born,
A shaggy sheepdog chasing the straying sheep,
The colour of the page that I am writing on.

Black and white:
A zebra crossing to keep pedestrians safe,
A zebra itself, scampering away from a fierce lion,
Chess pieces when they go into battle,
Crows and doves protecting their young,
Darkness and light.

Harry Edwards (13)
The Oratory School

THOUGHTS

It often frustrates me that adults ask me,
'What do you want to be when you're old and six feet tall?'
And though it may be rude to say, I wonder to myself,
What their reply would be if I asked them,
'What would you want to be if you were four years old
and very, very small?'

Zayn Sheikh (13)
The Oratory School

BRAIN-DEAD TED

He's Brain-Dead Ted
Sitting in my room inside my bed
He's my little snuggle bunny
He's Brain-Dead Ted

Lying on the floor with his voice inside my head
He's my lovey-dovey
He's Brain-Dead Ted

Doing my homework, writing with lead
He's my little shnuckums
He's Brain-Dead Ted

I come home from school and inside my room,
'Where is Ted?
'Where is my Brain-Dead Ted?'

I look for him but there is no sign
But he will always be mine
Because he is Brain-Dead Ted.

Jack Williams (12)
The Oratory School

PRIMARY COLOURS

Red is a finger that's been pricked by a pen
The frightening colour of evil eyes
The heart of a rabbit vigorous when scared
A wreath of poppies in memory of war heroes
Being embarrassed when you've done something wrong.

Yellow daffodils glinting in the golden sun
Golden jewellery for a special occasion
Forked lightning flashing in the sky
Hay for a bed of a horse
A yellow banana skin, so easy to slip on.

The clear blue sky on a summer's morning
The wide blue sea, so much to explore
A tint of a kingfisher dashing for fish
The ink that is coming out of this pen
The blue wire on a bomb, should I cut it or not?

Liam Teasdale (12)
The Oratory School

PRIMARY COLOURS

Red:
The flame engulfing the innocent town,
The red needle pointing north,
The crazy man on the Tizer can,
The cherries on trees ready to eat,
The red pins holding up the posters
And the fiery depths of a volcano crater.

Yellow:
The glint of gold in the bank vault,
The burning sun high in the sky,
The powerful lion pouncing on its prey,
The banana gripped by the black gorilla,
The sunflower field shining bright,
The golden gladius in a Roman's hand.

Blue:
The raging sea capped with white,
The blue ink out of the pen,
The beautiful bluebells swaying in the breeze,
The blue sky looking on all,
The blue shark swimming in the deep,
The bluebird diving on the worm.

Sam Smith (12)
The Oratory School

School

The school day ends
The school day begins
A harsh punishment for our sins
First of all, double maths
Monday morning - we felt the teacher's wrath
Single biology where we study a tree
Why does this have to happen to me?
In chemistry we cook up a stench
Bonjour, now on to French
Now what's for lunch?
But I already have a hunch
Soggy cabbage and apple pie
The tower of sick bags reach the sky
They read out a list of names
There is no escaping double games
I wish I could hang that Turk
The one that invented work
At last, time for home
Then for some rest
For we have another test
That is the next day
It's a harsh way to pay.

Tim Perkin (14)
The Oratory School

Black And White

The nasty presence of a lonely night
A cold leather jacket, frozen like ice
The cries of a child who fears the dark
A winter night, pitch-black, with no moon or stars
The depths of space no one has seen.

The colour of light which keeps us warm
A single lily standing alone
The stars at night which light up the sky
A white morning cloud with a silver lining
And the ghost in your closet waiting to pounce.

Choongwe Steele (13)
The Oratory School

HAMBURGER HILL

Walking cautiously through the tall grass,
How strange it firstly seems.
The enemy approaches, 'Go, run fast!'
Shortly after, one sees the beams.

Rifles engage in serious crossfire,
The sky rapidly lights up.
American troops who lie in the mire,
Camouflaged in their green make-up.

A man is hit, 'Medic!' he screams,
While he falls to the bloody ground.
The medic arrives, too late it seems,
As the soldier ceases, to make a sound.

Suddenly, a man, a tall American man,
Fell, with a shout and a cry.
His legs, he saw, were not his anymore,
But the mud's and the grass's that lay high.

The shooting stops, the silence arrives,
Soldiers lie so still.
Along the ground, rifles and knives,
Welcome to Hamburger Hill.

Michael Roberts (13)
The Oratory School

PRIMARY COLOURS

Blue:
A peacock's feather springs to life,
A lonesome whale in the icy waters,
The sky behind the cluster of clouds,
The waves smooth out onto the beach,
Bluebells grasp onto the plants,
The ink coming out of this very pen.

Red:
The blood in a hard fought battle,
The sun setting after the long day,
A rose in the fresh morning air,
The colour of an infuriated face,
The sound of sirens in the air.

Yellow:
The rays of the bright sun,
Like the ripeness of the cornfields,
The mustard on a sizzling hot dog,
The soft golden sand along the beach,
The inside of a bitten apple,
A lone buttercup in the field.

Oliver Woodward (12)
The Oratory School

BLACK AND WHITE

White:
The joy on a small child's face,
The happiness of an old woman when she sees her grown-up child,
Bright white clouds on a sea of blue,
The dove bringing peace to countries torn apart by war.

Black:
Spreading disease and deceit,
Bringing war to peace-loving countries,
Turning father against son and mother against daughter.
On a canvas of pure white, black streaks cross, covering all in its path,
Will all fall before black or will white prevail?

Joe Coggrave (13)
The Oratory School

Black And White

Black:
The panther running into the night sky
As the blackbird swoops down,
The berry on the tree sways in the wind,
A cat is hunted as an unlucky charm
And a bat flutters from cave to cave.

White:
The frost as it settles on the ground,
The icing on a cake,
The early morning sun as it shines through the wind,
The polar bear as it hunts for fish in the dead, frozen lake
As the cold snowflakes land on its fur.

Black and white:
The two base colours entwined in old films,
A black cold desert,
A bandit riding through the night in the moon's path,
A chess board,
The night into day.

Alex Zarecky (13)
The Oratory School

My Dog

My dog is called Harvey
And he is a well meaning looking chap
But he is not what he seems.

For although he looks balanced
Through and through
All black and white
Sometimes I fear that it is his
Darker side which is true.

But maybe it is just when I am around
For I am told that he is
A well behaved hound.

Robert Keddie (14)
The Oratory School

Sleep

The world leaves you
Your mind weaves you
A life of myth and magic

Man deformed
Life reformed
A story to be told
The wonder to unfold

The future be foretold
The past unrolled
Life in the weave.

Huw Twiston Davies (13)
The Oratory School

THE FOREST

The forest is quiet
Cold
And dark.

The trees are tall
Green
And strong.

The night sky brings streaks of light through the trees
It makes the forest alive
Creatures of all sorts crawl the earth
And settle on their prey.

The forest seems empty
It feels harmless
But the night is alive.

Charlie Ingall (13)
The Oratory School

THE WOODS

The woods is a dark and peaceful place
Where animals of all kinds live and hibernate
A kingdom that holds valiant living things
That has kept us alive unto this very day
The woods is a place that changes from time to time
That holds a different scene that God has created
A place where the surroundings are unknown
And a place where people do not dwell
The sky is dark and shadows are bold
That gives animals and plants something to behold
A place that holds peace to everyone.

Daniel Housego (14)
The Oratory School

WINTER

Winter's coming you must beware
It's going to snow, time to prepare
It is soon going to be very cold
No going out unless you are bold

The snow fell down
Down to the ground
Where it lay
All night and day

All the lakes began to freeze
And the trees shook in a cold breeze
Everyone shuts their door
As snow begins to pour

Then it gets hot
And snow there is not
The cold has now gone
Because the sun has shone.

Tom Hinton (14)
The Oratory School

THE OCEAN

The ripples of life kissing the shore,
The lisps of waves hitting the moor,
The calmness that has confused sailors galore,
The timeless glow of the ocean's floor,
The reflector of the world's splendour,
But inside is an awful boar,
Who rips the life from victims unsure.

Alex Wheatley (13)
The Oratory School

WINTER

Mother Nature called down to Earth,
'Prepare yourselves for snow, sleet and hail,
For all the elements are going to bail,
Because to winter I will soon give birth.'

She whom never to be doubted, was right!
For on that very day
All the warmth went away
And left it clear for a superlative night.

That night she came
With winter at her heel
And to her everything had to kneel,
For she was their master, the one who came.

Then she let winter go
And my gosh, she had trained it well!
The snow fell
And all the elements were let blow.

In the morning the sight was stunning,
The frost sparkled on the trees,
The chill gripped to the children's knees,
The lakes were the best, very cunning.

Thomas Thurston (13)
The Oratory School

THE NEWS

On the lunchtime news from the BBC
Are so many tales of human misery.
A suicide bomber has blown up a shop
Killing three children - when will it stop?
A man in the States has gone mad with a gun
Shooting indiscriminately, killing everyone.
But then there's a hostage who's just been set free
On the lunchtime news from the BBC.

On the six o'clock news from the BBC
A serial killer is found guilty.
An old lady is battered about the head
For just 50p - they left her for dead.
Many countries in Europe have been flooded out,
While in parts of Africa they are suffering from drought.
But Leeds beat Southampton by four goals to three
On the six o'clock news from the BBC.

On the ten o'clock news from the BBC
Are terrorists claiming to be holy.
The Americans want to invade Iraq
But the Arabs will then want to fight back.
Two girls are found dead, their bodies abused;
A town is in mourning, angry, confused.
Then they give the result of the lottery
On the ten o'clock news from the BBC.

Oliver Berger (13)
The Oratory School

Mars

Mars is the coolest place to be.
People think the people there are
Green,
Horrible,
Slimy
And have big eyes.
But actually they are
Purple,
Kind,
Have three small eyes,
One head,
Which is part of the body,
Which has four arms
And two legs.
I know
'Cause I've been there!

Hugo Vaux (9)
The Oratory School

His Mind . . .

His mind is swirling into infinity,
Wondering when it will all stop,
If it is meant to go on forever,
Where do you go when it is all over?
Do you go into outer space
And wonder if you will find a place to stay forever?
Or will you go to a happy place
And be in ecstasy for eternity?
The end is confusing,
The end of life.

Hamish Carr (13)
The Oratory School

BLACK AND WHITE

Black is a memory of death oozing its way through the shadows
Watching, waiting, keeping an eye open for a victim
It scares the wits out of us, making us careless
And that's when we slip into the shadow of its cloak
And it engulfs us, as a snake would gobble up its prey
We are fearful of it, but in a way, it can help us.

White is a gift, it brings out the beauty of an angel
It guides us and gives us hope
It's the colour of a dove and the sign of peace
Without it we would be lost
White is the colour of the snow, beautiful yet deadly
It is what gives the Alps its beauty.

Joshua Woodeson (13)
The Oratory School

BUILD UP

Out of the tunnel the warriors march;
palms sweatin', adrenaline pounding.
Undercover from the lights,
you turn to skills you've taken weeks to master.
All the buckets of sweat you have given for your place,
which would fall to nothing if all breaks
in the next ninety minutes of war.

A thousand eyes witnessing your moment of glory,
pride and honour.
The musketeers spring to mind as you gaze at your army
as they tune into their psyche which will pull through
their battering and wounds.

Joe Woodward (13)
The Oratory School

PRIMARY COLOURS

The blood of a murdered king,
The rose with its sharp prickles,
The war-like poppy,
A beautiful colour in the rainbow,
The red sea,
The pretty rose,
Red can be war-like
But also gentle.

The dark sea,
A gentle pool,
Bluebells sitting,
The fourth colour in the rainbow,
A pair of blue eyes,
A sign of good looks,
A gentle colour,
Blue.

The beautiful daffodil,
The autumn leaves,
A butterfly's shaded wings,
The brightest colour in the rainbow,
The colour nearest to gold,
The sun's rays,
An environmental colour,
Yellow.

Jack Hudson (12)
The Oratory School

The News

Monday:
A bomb explodes - hundreds dead
Citizens tremble before the threat.
A famine strikes - children suffer
Africa's future is in trouble.
A river floods - a city ruined
Brave firemen rush in to help the wounded.
A celebrity's wife gives birth to a son
A new life is born, opportunities to come.

Wednesday:
The deceased are found - their bodies recovered
Doctors rush in to help the others.
The famine is helped - rain falls from the sky
New roots are born for crops to thrive.
The floods have stopped - buildings are ruined
Nobody dead but many wounded.
The child is named but still unseen
The media rush to the scene.

Friday:
A ceremony is held to remember the dead
People become aware of the imminent threat.
The famine is over as crops have sprung
Humans have survived nature's thump.
Buildings repaired - a city is saved
People now prepared for the same.

Jonathan Wright (13)
The Oratory School

THE DIVING BELL AND THE BUTTERFLY

I was born a healthy child, just like any other.
I had a normal child life, I was a rebellious teenager.
When I was 21 I was involved in an accident.
I still remember the wailing screech of the tyres as I fought
to regain control of my car.
I didn't - I crashed and the metallic crunching of metal still echoes
through my head as I recall the incident.
As I ploughed through a clump of trees by the roadside
I remember thinking, *Is this it?*
I thought it was.
But, to my astonishment and overwhelming relief.
I woke up later that week in hospital.
They said I'd been in a coma for a few days.
I felt relieved, I sat up in bed, or at least I tried to,
I couldn't, I just couldn't. My body was not responding,
I just laid there for a few minutes.
I tried feverishly to wiggle my toes, I couldn't,
I was *paralysed!*

I have been paralysed for nearly 10 years and I've got used to
the boredom a bit.
I wish, with all my heart, that this curse would be undone or healed,
But it can't.
My body feels like a diving bell.
It is pulling me down, restricting movement and decreasing
the things I can do.
My soul is a butterfly but is being pulled down from the light of life
and down to the black hell that is paralysis.
I wish I could cut out the word holding them together,
I wish I could unbind them . . .
But I can't, and it haunts me every day of my life!

Jonathan Crowley (13)
The Oratory School

WHAT'S THE MEANING?

Beaten women hide and cry, running from abuse,
Crying children that know they've been misused,
Broken hearts they say will never mend,
What's round the corner, what's their end?
    It's their lives,
    Won't anyone let them know,
    Their lives, will anyone let them go?
Hungry families, desperate for money, for rent,
Running low on luck, the good life is spent.
Once friendly neighbours, wealthy their accounts soared,
Now they're low lives, all the meaning of money has been absorbed.
    It's their lives,
    It's all a panic game,
    Life is luck you know,
    We're all the same.
War and death, isn't all the same at times,
Terrorism is evil but what about crimes?
Killer leaders sending soldiers into mayhem,
Falling into darkness, who will save them?
    It's our lives,
    Don't forget the futile war,
    Breaking rules and crushing laws,
    Lives at last, spirits free,
    Free to rethink, let them be.
So sing a happy song,
Abuse all the others,
With money you are strong,
Forget about your brothers,
But in the end, who are you believing?
Tell me now, do you know the meaning . . . (of life?)

Simon Delfosse (13)
The Oratory School

Where Is It?

Here I stand on the battlefield,
Death facing me,
Destruction past me,
I wield a weapon of death,
But I gain nothing.

Now I fly among the stars,
Past nebulas, past black holes.
In a vessel that could destroy planets,
I choose who lives and who dies.
But I still gain nothing.

I stand beside trees,
In a place unknown.
'I want to gain something,' I shout.
But no.

Nothing, emptiness, oblivion.
I listen harder but no,
'Why?
I did what you said.'
Silence.

I see myself
Travelling the river of time,
Not knowing what to expect,
Not knowing what to do.

'Why?'
Someone speaks.
'When silence listens to silences,
All that you shall see
Is the darkness that binds you
And only you can set it free.'

'How?' I say but silence answers me.

G Benipal (14)
Wexham School

WAR

When he gets to Heaven
To Saint Peter he will tell
One more soldier reporting sir
I will serve my time in Hell.

Toward the blooded grass
There lay the foul stench of the motionless
The grasp of pistols and lifeless
Never in my life have I seen so many dead.

The water is red with sickness
The beach is black with anger
The rocks are tragic with dusts
The lost of thousands for wives and mothers.

The war has taken many far away
For those who are alive perish every day
The screams and gunfire they hear every time they pray
To live and tell the tale to grandchildren
To those who survive the First World War.

John Childs (13)
Wexham School

BLUE

Vast regions of silvery stars embrace the indigo midnight sky,
Within it lies this pale blue light,
For it is the azure moon,
Filled with soothing tranquil,
It is singing a graceful melody to the blanket of sapphire,
Crystal clear waters,
A shimmering light glows evermore,
Showering down the ocean floor,
The serenade of water.

Vishal Satwani (13)
Wexham School